LIFE LESSONS FROM GOD

Michele Hayes-Grisham

WESTBOW
PRESS
A DIVISION OF THOMAS NELSON

WestBow Press books may be ordered through booksellers or by contacting:

WestBow Press
A Division of Thomas Nelson
1663 Liberty Drive
Bloomington, IN 47403
www.westbowpress.com
1-(866) 928-1240

ISBN: 978-1-4497-5082-4 (sc)
ISBN: 978-1-4497-5083-1 (e)
Library of Congress Control Number: 2012908111

Printed in the United States of America

WestBow Press rev. date: 07/30/2012

CONTENTS

Introduction		vii
Acknowledgments		xi
Chapter 1	Miracles from God	1
Chapter 2	Love	11
Chapter 3	Forgiveness	15
Chapter 4	Self-control	22
Chapter 5	Perseverance	25
Chapter 6	Self-worth and Confidence	33
Chapter 7	Guilt and Shame	38
Chapter 8	Being a Good Steward of Time, Energy & Money	44
Chapter 9	Fear	57
Chapter 10	Relationships	62
Chapter 11	Health, Illness & Pain	72
Chapter 12	Contentment & Joy	83
Chapter 13	Dare to Care	94
Chapter 14	What was I thinking?	98
Chapter 15	Your Savior, Mentor & Friend	104
Notes		107
Abbreviations		109
Resources		111

INTRODUCTION

This book was written to encourage you when you become discouraged. Life can be hard, a real roller coaster, but you can have peace and joy in your life that makes every day special. I have had many joys and adventures and many sorrows and pain; but Jesus has been with me through all of them.

He is as real now as the days he walked in Jerusalem. There are more books written about Him and the evidence of His life than any other person who lived on this earth. His power and love remain with us in the form of the Holy Spirit. Not everyone has the Holy Spirit in them because you have to invite Him in. He does not force His way in, but lovingly and patiently knocks on the door of your heart asking to come in. Ask any Christian who is passionately seeking to follow Jesus and His will for their life; there is a difference when we ask Jesus into our hearts, minds, and lives.

There is no mystery in what we are to do or how we are to do it. God did not leave us with a quick love note, but a novel of love, drama, history and amazement called the Bible. The Bible tells us if we seek Him, we will find Him (1 Chronicles 28:9). If you come near to God, He will come near to you (James 4:8). The Bible is God's guide for our lives. Each commandment He gives us is because He loves us. Not one of them is to stop us from having fun, but on the contrary is to keep us from hurting ourselves or others. God's way is always the right way.

I have known three lovely young women who needlessly died because they gave up on themselves. They realized they had strayed from the path they should have been walking, and in guilt and shame; their lives were ended. My heart aches for the lives they could have had. God's grace and mercy are new every morning. It is never too late to start over again. There are people and places waiting to help you. Churches, Rescue Missions and many programs are in the business of giving hope to the hopeless.

Maybe you feel your family and friends have turned their backs on you. Sometimes love must be tough when you have consistently done things which are detrimental to yourself and to others. If you have been living in a way that is harmful to yourself and those around you, you have to find a new way to live. The gospel is the good news that Jesus died for sinners like you and me. Jesus can give you the courage and strength to start your life over.

This may not be the first time you have disappointed yourself and others, but get up and try again to live life as God intended. You will find that God's ways may not be the easiest, but they are the best. Maybe you are embarrassed by what you have done in the past; but you can have a new future. In the Bible, there were times when peoples' lives were so completely changed that God gave them a new name. He can do that for you. Turn your back on the old ways that caused heartache and pain and learn to reflect the light of Jesus in the darkness and be salt to preserve what is good. Be who God created you to be.

Don't give up on yourself. God doesn't give up on you!

ACKNOWLEDGMENTS

I would like to thank the ladies I have met and shared life with at the House of Hope. In my years of coming to encourage and bless you, I have been blessed. The time I have spent with women of all ages and cultures has shown me that there are always more things we share that connect us than the differences that separate us. Your kindness and love is always appreciated.

My husband, John, has graciously accepted the countless hours it took me to compose these stories and bits of wisdom to share with you.

My daughter, Tracy, is the beat of my heart and has always been so loving, encouraging and caring through this roller coaster we call life.

Life is so much better when we can share the joys and trials. A big thank you goes to my family and friends for helping to make my life so much richer.

CHAPTER 1
MIRACLES FROM GOD

Sometimes when heartbreaking events occur in our lives we wonder how a loving God could have allowed them to happen. When our second daughter died 5 ½ months into my pregnancy, it didn't seem possible that God would allow that. My pregnancy had had problems, but as an optimistic person, I was sure that our baby would be fine.

The device that was supposed to have prevented me from getting pregnant (a CU7) had dislodged. When I found I was pregnant and the doctor tried to remove it, it recoiled with a slingshot affect, and moved up into the uterus instead of coming out. I was told that I only had a 50% chance of carrying our baby to term, but I was sure we would be in the positive 50%. During the pregnancy there had been spotting and I was hospitalized to try to prevent a miscarriage from occurring.

My husband, John, knew I was having a hard time after the second hospital stay and suggested we travel to visit his cousins. I love people and my spirits are always raised when we can spend time with family and friends. I was feeling fine and had gone to the restroom before we left to take the kids to the zoo. My umbilical cord had been severed by the CU7 and was exposed when I went to the restroom. I was taken to a nearby hospital and was told the baby was dead, but I was so far along in the pregnancy that I would need to go through labor and deliver our stillborn child.

This delivery was so different than when our first daughter was born. There was no gathering of happy family with smiles and cheer. I was put in a room with a nurse monitoring me. The doctor came in and our tiny daughter was delivered. I wasn't given the opportunity to hold her or name her. She was placed in a bed pan and I was allowed a short time to stare at the tiny but perfect baby. I saw all the tiny fingers and toes and her little button nose. She was perfect. Our daughter was whisked away and I was taken to surgery because the placenta had not delivered. It was late at night and my husband had already gone to put our other daughter, Tracy, to bed at his cousin's home.

The hospital was crowded and the only available room had one adjoining wall connected to the nursery. I could hear the other babies and the oohs and aahs of the new parents and grandparents. When I was returned to my room, I cried for the child I would never know. A kind nurse came in and comforted me and reminded me of the blessing I had by already having another child to love. I was thankful, but I was also so sad that I would never get to know our second daughter and watch all the firsts of her life.

John arrived early the next morning to help me prepare to leave the hospital. His cousins were so kind and compassionate and offered to let me recuperate there while John returned home to work. I declined because I just wanted to be home.

John took me to his Mother's home to stay for the first day. She was compassionate, but it seemed like everything went back to normal with me driving to our house to get a change of clothes while my mother-in-law watched Tracy. I only had maternity clothes in my suitcase and it was agony to put them back on.

My husband was very kind and caring, but as with many people, his attitude was to not think about sad things and move on. I tried, but the grief of losing our daughter filled me with sadness and despair. There was no funeral, no grave, and no baby to hold and love. There was a giant hole in my heart that would not heal.

I know all this seems so depressing, but I write this that you might know that God can heal all wounds and just as Romans 8:28 says, *"And we know that in all things God works for the good of those who love him, who have been called according to his purpose."* Even the loss of a child can provide positive opportunities to change your life and those around you.

God did not cause our daughter to die, but He did allow it. I know that God loves my children even more than I, and so I have learned to accept that He is sovereign even when I cannot understand. There were several years of a longing ache that seemed would never be gone. As a mom, I pondered what happens when a baby dies. There was the not knowing and a great sadness that lingered. I realize now, they are immediately ushered into God's presence when they die because they have no sins to forgive and no scars or guilt from life.

One night as I drifted off to sleep with a restless sadness that had not gone away, God let me awake in heaven. It was just as the Bible says, ". . . *Now I know in part; then I shall know fully, even as I am fully known.*" (1 Corinthians. 13:12). Running joyfully toward me was our daughter. She was happy and glowing with love. She said, "Mommy, Mommy, don't be sad. I am fine. I love you so much! Pappaw is here and it is so beautiful! You will love it! Please don't be unhappy." Then she stood still and smiled at me. Even though I was suspended above the ground and unable to touch her, her love seemed to surround me like a warm hug. I was so full of joy that even when I was immediately returned to earth and my bed, the warmth of her love and joy still surrounded me.

I have never felt sorrow about her since. There are times I feel the loss of missing her, but now it is with joyful anticipation. God gave me the peace and joy I had been missing since our daughter died.

A couple of weeks later I went to a Christian bookstore to purchase some books I had been wanting. After the young girl rang up my books, she handed me a brown paper grab bag. The store was closing out a section of their store and giving away grab bags with each purchase. I carried the bag and books to my car and opened the bag.

Inside was a round, porcelain painted picture surrounded by pink lace with a magnet attached on the back. It was a perfect portrait of our daughter in heaven. She had the same beautiful smile and natural curly hair like her Grandma Lois. She was surrounded by the same gorgeous flowers and wearing the same cute jumper I had seen in heaven. Her portrait now graces our refrigerator door next to a picture of her older sister, Tracy. God had given me a special reminder.

A few years ago I was home alone. I was walking down the hall past the family pictures. I was talking out loud to God, and said to Him, "I wish I could've named our daughter. I tell people I have one daughter in heaven and one on earth; but I have no name for her." Then I felt a vibration in every cell in my body and in my home. With an audible, deep, gentle voice God told me, "I named her. Her name is Sally." It was so unexpected, yet so totally comforting. There was an awesome sense of joy and peace that filled my soul. How could I have thought that God would not take care of my daughter's every need? The Bible tells us that God is, *"A father to the fatherless, a defender of widows, is God in his holy dwelling."* (Psalm 68:5).

I stopped motionless, so amazed that God cared about the ache in my heart for the child I had never held. The love and compassion that He showed me about the detail that had lingered in my mind was hard to comprehend; a name for my child. Sally was not one of the names I had chosen from the baby book of names, and I wondered why God had chosen that name. I know God cares about every detail of our lives, so I knew there must be a reason.

I googled, "Sally meaning of name," on the internet. Sally is the English form of the Hebrew name Sarah which means "princess, or daughter of the king". Our Sally is indeed a daughter of the king. God is the father to the orphan and any child that enters heaven. She has a big brother, Jesus, and she will never know pain, heartache or guilt.

As the years fly by and my hair turns gray, I grow nearer to the time that I will be reunited with our daughter, Sally. Death now has not only lost its sting, but I know that death from this life will begin my perfect life with our daughter in heaven. Ageing no longer has a negative effect on me, but a positive one. Getting older just means I'm closer to seeing those I love who have gone to heaven before me. If you have any doubt that God is still active and alive in our lives, just ask any Christian who passionately seeks Him. The Bible teaches us, ". . . *The LORD is with you when you are with him. If you seek him, he will be found by you, but if you forsake him, he will forsake you.* (2 Chronicles 15:2). God does not force His way into our lives.

People are still being healed and demons cast out. We shy away from what we do not understand, but when you read and pray and begin to know Him, you will be drawn more and more to understand Him and His will for your life. *"In the last days, God says, I will pour out my Spirit on all people. Your sons and daughters will prophesy, your young men will see visions, your old men will dream dreams.* (Acts 2:17).

I believe part of the reason we have a hard time hearing Him speak to us is our hectic lifestyles. The times I have heard Him most clearly are when I am alone with no television or radio to distract me. I have learned to praise and thank Him, pour out my heart; and then just listen. In order to be able to trust that what you hear is from Him, test it against what the Bible says about His character.

His voice will never lead us to do anything that is contrary to what the Bible says. Sometimes there is a voice and sometimes it is a thought that comes into your mind and you know it wasn't your idea because it is a thought far superior to your own.

It is imperative that we know what the Bible says so that we will not be led astray. I remember hearing a preacher say that drinking alcohol was a sin. Think about that. Would Jesus have turned the water into wine if drinking was a sin? In Proverbs 23:20-21 we read, *"Do not join those who drink too much wine or gorge themselves on meat, for drunkards and gluttons become poor, and drowsiness clothes them in rags."* Also, the Bible does say in 1 Timothy 5:23, *"Stop drinking only water, and use a little wine because of your stomach and your frequent illnesses."*

The sin is not drinking wine, but becoming drunk. Did you notice it also talked about eating too much? When we do not understand moderation, we begin to live a life that is out of balance.

Another example of how people can be led astray is the horrendous story of Jim Jones and his followers. In November 1978, he and over 900 of his followers committed suicide in Jonestown, Guyana by drinking poisoned Flavor Aid. Now, as in Biblical times, there are people who teach things that are contrary to what Jesus taught and what the word of God says. As Jesus said, *"I am sending you out like sheep among wolves. Therefore be as shrewd as snakes and as innocent as doves."* (Matthew 10:16).

When you have asked the Holy Spirit to come into your life, and as your walk with Jesus deepens; you will begin to hear those still small whispers guiding you in an act of service or a word of encouragement to someone. The Bible tells us there will be times when God does not answer us as we would like Him to. *"When you ask, you do not receive, because you ask with wrong motives, that you may spend what you get on your pleasures."* (James 4:3).

Don't forget that God's timing is not ours. He might say yes, no, or not yet. There are many stories in the Bible that show some of God's promises took years, decades or even centuries to be fulfilled.

Have you ever heard it said that the Bible is God's living and breathing word? What that means is that no matter how many times you have read it, you will always find something new that speaks to you. Some verses that don't seem to apply to you now may one day be exactly what you need to hear.

In 2011 I had the wonderful opportunity to go to Zambia, Africa with my missionary friend, Barbara, and other friends from church. Barbara and her husband had started helping widows and orphans years before and had established a mission school, two schools for the deaf and continue to help provide care for over 600 orphans. I thought my primary service in going would be to love kids, but Barbara asked if I would also speak to the women to encourage them as she had heard me encourage the women at our homeless shelter. I was happy to do that.

We hadn't been in Zambia long and we were all very jet lagged. Three of us had laid down to take a nap. I was very tired, but I heard the Holy Spirit tell me, "Go outside and teach." I knew that thought was not mine, because I really thought sleep would be a good idea. I took my Bible and went outside to sit on the porch.

I thought that some child or woman would probably come by and talk with me. Instead, a young man in training for the pastorate came. He walked up and asked if Pastor Mulenga was home. I said he was not and introduced myself.

He asked what I was reading and I told him Isaiah, as that was what we were studying in Bible Study Fellowship. He asked what I thought about what I was reading. I said I thought that Isaiah was such an encouraging book. He said it had been troubling him that God had used Babylon, a nation who did not follow God, to punish God's own people for their sinfulness. I am thankful I had studied those verses with the 18 ladies in my group, because I knew how each of us had learned something that the others had missed. In Isaiah 47:6-7 it says, *"I was angry with my people and desecrated my inheritance; I gave them into your [Babylon's] hand, and you showed them no mercy. Even on the aged you laid a very heavy yoke. You said, 'I will continue forever—the eternal queen!' But you did not consider these things or reflect on what might happen."*

God had warned the Israelites through the prophets of Israel's downfall, but the people did not listen. God allowed Babylon to capture Jerusalem and take the people captive. However, God punished Babylon for her cruelty.

When we feel like the world is out of control and God is not taking care of things, we are so wrong. We do not see the big and eternal picture. God told us we would have troubles, but He will never leave us or forsake us. As the father allows the rod to lovingly correct a beloved child; so God uses trials to mold us and shape us into humble usable instruments for His love. God cared about that young man's concern about why a loving God would allow His people to be conquered by a wicked nation. By sharing what we learn, we are able to encourage others (it doesn't matter who they are or where they live). When God tells you to do something; do it. You will be blessed and be a blessing to others.

CHAPTER 2
LOVE

What words of wisdom does God give us to guide our lives? We have a huge manual from Him called the Bible. Jesus simplified it when he answered a Pharisee who asked, *"Teacher, which is the greatest commandment in the Law?" Jesus replied; "Love the Lord your God with all your heart and with all your soul and with all your mind. This is the first and greatest commandment. And the second is like it: Love your neighbor as yourself. All the Law and the Prophets hang on these two commandments."*(Matthew 22:36-40).

So what does this mean for us? It is when we study God's words in the Bible that we begin to comprehend how great and loving He is. When you accept God as the creator of everything and your maker; you realize He is true love and wisdom personified. He does have the wisdom, right, and authority to tell us how to best live our lives. It was not until the birth of Jesus and His death on the cross that we realized the depth of God's love for mankind. In spite of all we have done, He woos us to Himself. He does not give up on us, and Jesus tells us in Luke 15:7, *"I tell you that in the same way there will be more rejoicing in heaven over one sinner who repents than over ninety-nine righteous persons who do not need to repent.*" God is faithful and yearns for the return of His prodigals.

As you learn of the love, grace and mercy that God lavishes on us, His children; loving Him is so easy and natural. Like the song says, "When you can't see His hand, trust His heart."

It is often much harder to love our neighbor, spouse or co-worker. Many of our problems with others are misunderstandings and miscommunications. I have met very few people who have a life mission of making others miserable. It is usually when we are thinking about our own life and problems that we are not open to any conversation. We may be unconsciously so self-absorbed that any communication from someone feels like an unwanted intrusion. We very likely have no anger or ill will towards them, but our gruff response is understandably received in a negative light. Our perception is not always correct.

One of my favorite sayings is, "Do not judge someone if you have not walked a mile in their moccasins." Since we have not lived anyone else's life, we don't truly know the circumstances that have shaped their lives and thinking. Why people are the way they are is a complex combination of genetics and life experiences. Even though their lifestyle may not be such that we socialize regularly with them, in the time we do interact, we can be kind, caring and nonjudgmental, just as Jesus was. Sometimes we may feel that we are not able to concentrate on being a good Christian because we are so busy and rushed. We think we don't have the time, money or training to perform acts of love. God does not ask us to accomplish massive projects or interact with dozens of people. To the contrary, God says, *"If I have the gift of prophecy and can fathom all mysteries and all knowledge, and if I have a faith that can move mountains, but have not love, I am nothing. If I give all I possess to the poor and surrender my body to the flames, but have not love, I gain nothing."* (1 Corinthians 13:2-3).

It is not as important that we achieve great things or give away our material possessions as it is that we just love people. In 1 Peter 4:8 we read, *"Above all, love each other deeply, because love covers over a multitude of sins."*

In the advertising world, it seems like love is a new car or a diamond, but those items aren't even listed in what God says love is. God says, *"Love is patient, love is kind. It does not envy, it does not boast, it is not proud. It is not rude, it is not self-seeking, it is not easily angered, it keeps no record of wrongs. Love does not delight in evil but rejoices with the truth. It always protects, always trusts, always hopes, always perseveres. Love never fails."* (1 Corinthians 13:4-8a). Love is about how we treat someone, not what material possessions we give them. In addition to loving someone, we may choose to express our love by giving them gifts or money or providing shelter or support.

If you have not been raised in a loving home, maybe you don't even know what love looks like. Read the list again telling us what God says love is. Developing new habits is possible. If there is a particular area that you struggle with, there are many good Christian books that will help strengthen those areas that are hard for you. Whether it is an issue with anger, trust, or self-control;

there are books and Christian professionals just waiting to help you overcome that weakness.

A prayer that has helped me immensely is, "Dear God, please help me to see with your eyes, speak with your heart and be your hands and feet." Only God can change a heart. The Bible says, "*You want something but don't get it. You kill and covet, but you cannot have what you want. You quarrel and fight. You do not have, because you do not ask God. When you ask, you do not receive, because you ask with wrong motives, that you may spend what you get on your pleasures.*" (James 4:2-3).

Just wanting something is not enough. It has to be something that is in God's will. God is not a genie waiting for our commands. God is a wise and loving Father that wants only the best for His children.

CHAPTER 3
FORGIVENESS

Forgiveness is something we all want to receive, but it is sometimes so hard to give. Some hurts are easy to forgive, but others seem impossible. A wise Christian counselor explained to me that we usually find it relatively easy to forgive a sin that we think we might commit, but it is much harder to forgive a sin that we think we would never commit. As James 2:10 says, *"For whoever keeps the whole law and yet stumbles at just one point is guilty of breaking all of it."* We have all sinned and we all want to be forgiven.

When we disobey a commandment, we violate the will of God. It is when deep, crushing hurts happen that it is beneficial to seek help to get through them. When a grievous sin occurs it is often by someone we loved and trusted, and that is why it hurts so much. Sometimes forgiveness requires consistent prayer and positive actions on our part before positive feelings return.

God does not instruct us to forgive others just to benefit those we forgive, but it is also to release our bitterness and anger that can linger like an infected wound. Matthew 6:14-15 tells us, *"For if you forgive men when they sin against you, your heavenly Father will also forgive you. But if you do not forgive men their sins, your Father will not forgive your sins."*

There is a condition involved as it states in Luke 17:3. *"... If your brother sins, rebuke him,* [strong expression of disapproval] *and if he repents, forgive him."* So what does it mean for them to repent? According to the notes in the NIV Study Bible for Matthew 3:2, "Repentance is not merely a change of mind but a radical change in one's life as a whole that especially involves forsaking sin and turning or returning to God."

Luke 13:3 reads, *"... But unless you repent, you too will all perish."* We cannot know if someone is truly repentant, because only God knows what is in a person's heart. As 1 Corinthians 4:3-5 states, *"I care very little if I am judged by you or by any human court; indeed, I do not even judge myself. My conscience is clear, but that does not make me innocent. It is the Lord who judges me. Therefore judge nothing before the appointed time; wait till the Lord comes. He will bring to light what is hidden in darkness and will expose the motives of men's hearts. At that time each will receive his praise from God."*

We need not worry if someone will receive the punishment they deserve or the rewards. The Bible tells us that vengeance is God's. He can punish beyond what we can imagine and His punishment will be with an unrepentant sinner for eternity.

God especially cares about the little ones as the Bible says in Matthew 18:6, *"But if anyone causes one of these little ones who believe in me to sin, it would be better for him to have a large millstone hung around his neck and to be drowned in the depths of the sea."*

Never doubt that God sees and God cares. In Revelation 7:17 we read, *"For the Lamb at the center of the throne will be their shepherd; he will lead them to springs of living water. And God will wipe away every tear from their eyes."*

God will wipe our tears away Himself, it will not be done by an angel or seraphim; God will touch us personally. He is our Abba Father, Daddy. Our God will punish those who do evil and reward those things we do to show love and honor for Him.

Perhaps the best way to learn forgiveness is to be forgiven or see forgiveness in action. When I was in second grade, we had a new teacher. When it was my turn to read, there were words that I could not pronounce correctly. I had been born with a tied tongue. One of the words I could not pronounce correctly was school, and when I read it, I pronounced it "stool".

The teacher assumed that because I was the youngest of three children that I was just lazy and didn't try. She mimicked me by saying, "So you go to stool, do you?" I was extremely embarrassed and did not say anything more. On the bus ride home that night, the other kids started to tease me. Before the teacher had mimicked me, they either hadn't noticed my poor pronunciation skills or didn't think to tease me.

I got off the bus at home in tears and told my mom that I never wanted to go back to school again. When I told her what happened, she immediately drove back to the school and confronted the teacher. The teacher was very sorry for what she had done. She cried and apologized, but the damage was done. I vowed never again to speak in front of anyone unless I had to or until I knew them and felt safe. I kept that vow until I was in my mid-thirties.

(In chapter 6—Self-worth and Confidence, I'll tell you how God changed that.)

My family was very poor and we qualified to have free speech therapy at Indiana State University, but the 120 mile round trip was not possible with only one car for transportation. My mom bought phonics cards and most evenings we would work on repeating those hard sounds until my tongue could master them.

When we went to the monthly Parent/Teachers Association meeting, my mom found out this same teacher did not drive and always had to pay for a cab for her transportation. My mom offered to take her home after the meeting, and continued to drive her home every month. There is a song that says, "I'd rather see a sermon than to hear one any day." My mom's loving and giving spirit was such a good example for me.

My mom was also very self-conscious and went out of her way to make everyone feel welcome whenever possible. My family probably had the smallest house of all of our family and friends, but she always invited anyone who wanted to attend any gathering they had. She always had a house full that spilled out into the yard, but she loved it. When we moved to Arizona, we lived in a 12 by 60 foot house trailer; but it was usually the gathering place for the holidays. My mom was also the perfect model for what hospitality should look like. She left a legacy for me and many others that will help guide us throughout our lives.

In John 4:6-26, Jesus spoke to a Samaritan woman who came to a well to draw water. The woman led an adulteress life and was out at noon during the heat of the day, probably to avoid the disapproving glances and whispers of her community. In the culture of that time, it was not even acceptable for a man to speak with a woman who was a stranger. Jesus lived by the law of love, not of culture. Even though Jesus knew of her adulteress affairs, he saw through those poor choices to the heart of a woman searching for love and meaning in life.

Jesus had lived a perfect life and had the right and authority to verbally scold her; but He did not. He cared about her and knew the Samaritan culture she came from lacked much of the information God had given to the Jews. She knew her peers were in debate about where they should worship. Jesus explained that where you worshiped God was not important. What did matter was that God should be worshiped in spirit and in truth in all our thoughts and actions.

The truly amazing part of Jesus' interaction with this woman was that she was the first person He told He was the Messiah. In John 4:25-26, it reads, *"The woman said, "I know that Messiah" (called Christ) "is coming. When he comes, he will explain everything to us." Then Jesus declared, "I who speak to you am he."*

Wow! If we had met her, we might have thought that we shouldn't cast pearls before swine (Matthew 7:6). That is exactly why we should not judge others and decide if they are worthy of our time and efforts. God rewards our perseverance and it is He who will judge their hearts and if good fruit is produced by them.

When it is evident people are not open or respectful to our sharing about God, we shake the dust off our feet and move on (Matthew 10:14). Possibly a seed you have planted will bare fruit when another waters it.

How can we again love someone who has hurt us so deeply? Probably one of Satan's biggest lies to us is that if someone hurts us, they are a bad person or they don't love us. Good people can do wrong acts in their life. People can truly love us but still commit sins against us. Sin is usually a self-centered act and the people being affected very likely aren't even thought about during the sin. For me, the best example of this was King David.

The Bible in 2 Samuel 11 tells us that David was a man after God's own heart. How could this man of God be so envious of Uriah the Hittite's one wife when David had multiple wives? David compounded his sin because he tried to hide his immorality when Bathsheba became pregnant.

David ordered Uriah to come to him to report how the war was going as a guise to have him return home to make it look as if the baby to be was fathered by Uriah. Uriah was such an honorable man that he would not allow himself the luxuries and comforts of home when the men he was in charge of in the field of battle were denied. Uriah slept at the entrance to the palace with all his master's servants and did not go down to his house.

In a fit of anger and shame, David then had Uriah sent back into the worst area of the battle and then had Uriah's men retreat to ensure Uriah would be killed.

God had Nathan the prophet confront David with his sins. David confessed his sins and repented, but the child from that adulteress affair died in spite of David's pleadings to God. Did God forgive David for these sins? Yes, David was forgiven, but the consequences of those sins followed David and his children throughout the rest of their lives. It is likely David did not give strong guidance to his own children because of David's shame regarding his own sins.

Once again, God showed amazing love to David by allowing a later child of David and Bathsheba to be in the lineage leading to the birth of God's only son, Jesus. In Matthew 1:6 we read, *"David was the father of Solomon, whose mother had been Uriah's wife."* When you have sinned, and you think God could never use you again; remember David.

When we forgive others, we should forgive them like God forgives us. In Isaiah 43:25 we read, *"I, even I, am He who blots out your transgressions, for my own sake, and remembers your sins no more"*. I must admit that sometimes I don't blot out sins that someone commits against me. I just cover them with post-it notes so I can keep going back to them and feeling that pain and anger again. How silly is that? If God forgives us, what right do we have to hold those sins over each other indefinitely? We should forgive others like God forgives us. Throw away the post-it note covers and blot out those sins with permanent marking pens so we don't keep dredging them up.

CHAPTER 4
SELF-CONTROL

Proverbs 25:28 reads, *"Like a city whose walls are broken down is a man who lacks self-control."* This is one of the proverbs written by Solomon. Before we decide what self-control should look like, we'll review what the Bible says about it.

We need to have walls and boundaries. The world offers many choices and we have daily decisions to make. Sometimes good and bad are white and black, but sometimes Satan can make what is wrong look very good. A discerning heart questions not only what we decide but also why and when.

God does not withhold any good thing from His children, but He sees the big complete picture that we can't. When we earnestly seek His guidance, He will lead us. Even when we make poor decisions Romans 8:28 assures us that He will use it for our good. There may be consequences to suffer, but those too can be good reinforcements to remind us that God's way is always the best way.

Galatians 5:22-23 tells us, "The *fruit of the Spirit is love, joy, peace, patience, kindness, goodness, faithfulness, gentleness, and self-control. Against such things there is no law.*" The important thing to remember is that self-control is only one part of the fruit of the Spirit. True good and strong self-control is really depending on God-control (which is the Holy Spirit within us).

When we realize there is a sin nature within us, we must seek God and His words of wisdom to guide all our thoughts and actions. We recognize our weaknesses and accept that God in all His wisdom knows best. Especially when fighting an addiction; it takes us depending on God's strength and guidance to help us be able to do the right thing. No sin is ever worth the shame, pain and loss of self-respect that comes when we knowingly choose to do what we know is wrong; but still sometimes we fail. As 2 Timothy 3:3 tells us, "*Godlessness in the last days will include lack of self-control.*

Our nation is also destroyed by sin. In Proverbs 14:34 it reads, "*Righteousness exalts a nation, but sin is a disgrace to any people.*" We should pray not only for ourselves and others, but also for our leaders and our nation.

2 Peter 1:3-8 tells us if we want to receive a rich welcome into the eternal kingdom, "*His divine power has given us everything we need for life and godliness through our knowledge of Him who called us by His own glory and goodness. Through these He has given us His very great and precious promises, so that through them you may participate in the divine nature and escape the corruption in the world caused by evil desires. For this very reason make every effort to add to your faith goodness; and to goodness, knowledge; and to knowledge, self-control;*

and to self-control, perseverance; and to perseverance, godliness; and to godliness, brotherly kindness; and to brotherly kindness, love. For if you possess these qualities in increasing measure, they will keep you from being ineffective and unproductive in your knowledge of our Lord Jesus Christ."

When 1 Timothy 3:1-12 gives guidelines for Overseers [presiding officials] and deacons, it outlines the qualities for which mature godly Christians should strive. God does not want us to remain weak, baby Christians, but to grow in wisdom and love as it says in Hebrews 5:11-14. We cannot become Christ-like Christians if we do not know the word of God and live it in our daily lives.

As with any growth and maturing, it takes work and time. Our strength comes through prayer and learning the wisdom of God by reading the Bible. Hebrews 6:11-12 continues to say, *"We want each of you to show this same diligence to the very end, in order to make your hope sure. We do not want you to become lazy, but to imitate those who through faith and patience inherit what has been promised."*

What are some ways that our lives can show self-control? In 1 Timothy 2:8-10 we read, *"I want men everywhere to lift up holy hands in prayer, without anger or disputing. I also want women to dress modestly, with decency and propriety, not with braided hair or gold or pearls or expensive clothes, but with good deeds, appropriate for women who profess to worship God."* Being a Christian should be reflected in the way we act and dress.

In 1 Peter 1:13 it explains that as a Christian, there is an ongoing process for us to maintain, *"Therefore, prepare your minds for action; be self-controlled; set your hope fully on the grace to be given you when Jesus Christ is revealed."*

CHAPTER 5
PERSEVERANCE

Sometimes we may feel that no one sees or knows the problems that we are enduring in our lives. But, in Hebrews 12:1, we are told, *"Therefore, since we are surrounded by such a great cloud of witnesses, let us throw off everything that hinders and the sin that so easily entangles, and let us run with perseverance the race marked out for us."*

When we ask Jesus into our hearts and lives, He promises to always be with us and in us as the Holy Spirit guides us. Notice that the verse says we are surrounded by such a great cloud of witnesses. In your mind, think about being in a huge amphitheater. Imagine God, Jesus, the disciples, the martyrs and all the people you have loved in your life being there to cheer you on. Somehow when there are others yelling words of love and encouragement, we find a deep well within us that gives us the strength and courage to run a little farther. One of the most encouraging verses to me says that when we receive notice and attention for what we have done, and we do it for that honor; then that is all the reward we will receive.

However, if we live our lives to do our best at whatever chore is needed to be accomplished, as if we are serving Jesus himself; then we will have a reward waiting for us in heaven. Consider what is better, a trophy that will rust and accumulate dust, or an eternal reward from our Lord and Savior.

Matthew 6:2-4 reads, *"Be careful not to do your acts of righteousness before men, to be seen by them. If you do, you will have no reward from your Father in heaven. So when you give to the needy, do not announce it with trumpets, as the hypocrites do in the synagogues and on the streets, to be honored by men. I tell you the truth, they have received their reward in full. But when you give to the needy, do not let your left hand know what your right hand is doing, so that your giving may be in secret. Then your Father, who sees what is done in secret, will reward you."*

Did you notice it says, "the race marked out for us"? God does not send us running down a blind alley, but has a plan and map all marked out for us. It is not a race against anyone else, but it is our personal race. We cannot be Mother Teresa or Abraham Lincoln. God did not place us in their location or time in history. You cannot be anyone else; only the best you possible.

For most of us, our race is a long marathon, not a short sprint. If we want to be fit for the master's work, how do we plan for that? Daniel is probably the best example of how to be a good worker. He was offered royal food and wine, but he chose vegetables and water (Daniel chapter 1).

In life we have many decisions to make. We should care for our bodies because when we have accepted Jesus as our Savior and Lord, we receive the gift of the Holy Spirit to live within us. If we are to love, and give and achieve the works God has planned for us, we will need energy and endurance.

We sometimes forget to care for ourselves. It is admirable to want to do as much as possible for others; but Jesus modeled for us that we should also balance service with time with God (*Very early in the morning, while it was still dark, Jesus got up, left the house and went off to a solitary place, where he prayed."* (Mark 1:35); time away from the frenzy of life, (*Jesus, knowing that they intended to come and make him king by force, withdrew again to a mountain by himself."* (John 6:15); and time with family and friends (*When evening came, Jesus was reclining at the table with the Twelve."*(Matthew 26:20). We, too, are children of God, and are not to treat ourselves badly either. *"Don't you know that you yourselves are God's temple and that God's Spirit lives in you? If anyone destroys God's temple, God will destroy him; for God's temple is sacred, and you are that temple."* (1 Corinthians 3:16-17).

Because we have the Holy Spirit inside us, and are made in God's image; we should care for our bodies as well as to care for and love our neighbors. If we do not care for ourselves, we deplete our own bodies and no longer have the health and energy to care for others. I learned the hard way why we are to take time to care for ourselves.

Growing up I thought that I had to be perfect to be loved. When a teacher made fun of the way I talked in second grade, I decided I had to find a way to be perfect. My generation was the first that had television. We watched "Leave it to Beaver" and saw Mrs. Cleaver vacuuming her immaculate home in a dress and heels. In "Father Knows Best" we routinely saw any problem solved in 30 minutes or less. In perfume commercials they sang, "I can bring home the bacon, fry it up in a pan, and never let him forget he's a man."

Wow, what a tall order. Somehow I thought I should be able to work fulltime, keep our home as clean as our stay-at-home moms did, volunteer for every school activity our daughter was involved in, keep homemade cookies in the cookie jar, serve in various ways at the church and attend night school to complete my degree to go into nursing. I didn't let myself lie down at night until everything was done.

One weekend for our daughter's birthday, I took her and her friends to San Francisco to shop in the garment district. It was unusually hot there and that night in the motel I became very sick. It was probably the flu, but somehow I just couldn't recover. I could barely drag myself out of bed and my body had trouble even moving. Our doctor diagnosed my condition as "Chronic Fatigue Syndrome" or "Epstein Barr Virus". From everything I could find about it, there was no cure and people had suffered for decades with no improvement.

In some ways, what was even worse than the physical symptoms was that my brain seemed to be surrounded by a fog. My once sharp mind could now not even think of words like table or chair. My short term memory was hardly functioning. I had always graded myself on what I could accomplish, and now I could accomplish nothing. I had always been fairly optimistic, but now I felt I had no value and was a drain on my family. I felt strongly that my family would be far better off without me. I really thought that committing suicide would be best for everyone.

I was angry because I knew it was not me who should determine the length of my life. Psalm 139:16 says, *"All the days ordained for me were written in your book before one of them came to be."* I couldn't believe that the future held anything good.

There is a story in the book of Kings about Elijah the prophet who was fleeing from Jezebel. Elijah was afraid and ran for his life. He went into the desert, sat under a broom tree and prayed that he might die. Elijah said, *"I have had enough, Lord. Take my life; I am no better than my ancestors."* (I think all of us have had times when we thought, "I have had enough.") Elijah fell asleep and twice an angel of the Lord came and gave Elijah bread and water. The angel said to Elijah, *"Get up and eat, for the journey is too much for you." Strengthened by that food, he traveled forty days and forty nights until he reached Horeb, the mountain of God."* God had big plans for Elijah. Elijah persevered and was richly rewarded.

It was during the year I was bedridden that God taught me I had great value and He had given me everything I needed. In 1 Timothy 4:8 we learn, *"For physical training is of some value, but godliness has value for all things, holding promise for both the present life and the life to come."* Galatians 5:5 tells us, *"The only thing that counts is faith expressing itself through love."*

He spoke into my heart and mind that I could love my family, listen to them, and hug them. I could give my family the thing that was more important than anything I could do for them; I could love them.

I learned the importance of eating nutritious foods, sleeping the extra hours I needed, and exercising a little at a time to build my body back to functioning. I learned I have a weak immune system that probably started with being born premature (I weighed 3 pounds, 11 ounces at birth). I had to accept that nursing was not to be in my future.

When I was able to return to work, the head office notified me that I was being terminated after more than 13 years of service. I was blessed to be young enough to start over again. All of my co-workers were also gradually let go as our employer went through bankruptcy and a merger.

During the year that I was bedridden, I remember thinking that my future held no good thing ahead. That was when I was 34. Since that time, I completed 20 years of service with a new employer, watched our beautiful daughter marry a wonderful young man, and traveled to New Zealand, Israel, Africa, and Nicaragua. The trips to Africa and Nicaragua even allowed me to be of service to others.

God used the sickness, depression and pain to draw me closer to Him and to guide me into the service of encouragement to others for my Lord and Savior. He truly saved me from the pit of despair and has used all those negative times in my life to mold me into a more caring, compassionate and far less critical and judgmental person. God had to break me to make me into much more usable pottery. I would go through it all again because of the changes God has made in my heart and mind.

Another one of my favorite sayings is, "It doesn't matter how many times you fall down; it just matters that you keep getting back up." One interesting fact about millionaires is that many of them went through bankruptcy before becoming millionaires. Even three of our former U.S. Presidents had to go through bankruptcy. One of them was Abraham Lincoln. He had to file for bankruptcy not just once, but twice. It then took him 17 years to repay his family and friends (financialedge.investopedia.com).

You will never succeed if you are afraid to fail. It is from our failures that we can learn how to succeed. Don't give up! God does not give up on you.

One of my favorite songs is, "One Day at a Time". Isaiah 43:18 tells us not to be stuck in the past, it is past and cannot be changed; however, we can usually learn from our mistakes. We are not supposed to be anxious and worry about the future. I read a statistic that 40% of what we worry about never happens. What a waste of sleepless nights and acid churning stomachs. Mark Twain was quoted as saying, "Ninety-eight percent of what I worried about never happened." *"This is the day the Lord has made; let us rejoice and be glad in it."* (Psalm 118:24).

God will always be there with us throughout our struggles. Our future, if we have accepted Jesus as our Lord and Savior, is eternity in heaven with God and Jesus. The animals will all be tame and the children can play with them with no worries.

The world and Satan try to beat us down, not lift us up. In Hebrews 10:35-36 it says, *"So do not throw away your confidence; it will be richly rewarded. You need to persevere so that when you have done the will of God, you will receive what he has promised."* Don't give up or give in. Pray for strength in your times of weakness. I believe God does forgive those who in a time of crisis have taken their own lives; but what pain that leaves for those left behind. In John 10:28 Jesus says, *"I give them eternal life, and they shall never perish; no one can snatch them out of my hand."* Pain and depression can cause us to lose sight of the love and light our heavenly Father has for us.

A friend of mine committed suicide, and I have always wondered what I could have said or done to help her. I know I cannot help her by remembering that tragedy, but it does remind me to be vigilant to watch over those around me for signs that they are struggling. So much good has happened to my family and me since my struggle with depression and thoughts of suicide. God should be the one to determine when our time on earth ends. We can't see the big picture, but we can be confident of the future plans He has for us.

Once suicide occurs, the endless possibilities for God's love and blessings have ended in this life. God tells us in Jeremiah 29:11, *"For I know the plans I have for you," declares the LORD, "plans to prosper you and not to harm you, plans to give you hope and a future."*

CHAPTER 6
SELF-WORTH AND CONFIDENCE

"Oh yes, you shaped me first inside, then out; you formed me in my mother's womb. I thank you, High God—you're breathtaking! Body and soul, I am marvelously made! I worship in adoration—what a creation! You know me inside and out, you know every bone in my body; you know exactly how I was made, bit by bit, how I was sculpted from nothing into something. Like an open book, you watched me grow from conception to birth; all the stages of my life were spread out before you, the days of my life all prepared before I'd even lived one day." (Psalm 139:1-16) (The Message).

God created you, He loves you, and He sent his only son, Jesus, to die for you. Jesus died for you! You are **so** loved. *"God looked over everything he had made; it was so good, so very good!"* (Genesis 1:31) (The Message). You are one-of-a-kind. You are not supposed to be like anybody else; just you. I know when we have sinned that we don't feel worthy to be a child of God; but God is faithful to love us, forgive us, and woo us back to Him.

When we are down on ourselves, we remember only our failures. Think about this. The first time you try almost anything, you will not be good at it. The first time Hank Aaron hit a ball with his bat, it was probably not a homerun. From our first breath at birth until our last, we are experiencing new things. If we never try, we might not fail at that experience; but we will never succeed at anything.

God gave each of us talents and gifts, but we have to find out what those are. *"For we are God's workmanship, created in Christ Jesus to do good works, which God prepared in advance for us to do."* (Ephesians 2:10).

When you know you are one of God's creations, you should remember that you have great value, because God put it in you. There are books and websites that can help you discover what your spiritual gifts are.

When you are naturally gifted in a certain area, you may not recognize that as your gift. Because it comes easily to you, you might assume everyone finds it as easy as you do. Let's say you have the gift of hospitality. You know instinctively how to make people feel welcome and at ease. You are energized and look forward to having people come to your home. Many people suffer severe anxiety just thinking about the possibility of someone coming to their home.

You are far less likely to suffer burnout when you are serving in an area for which God has gifted you. We sometimes think that a gift we don't have is somehow better than ours or more important. The Bible teaches us that each part or gift is important and not to be looked down upon (1 Corinthians 12:12-26). You are important to God and your church body. Take your place and serve where God has gifted you.

"Now the body is not made up of one part but of many. If the foot should say, "Because I am not a hand, I do not belong to the body," it would not for that reason cease to be part of the body. And if the ear should say, "Because I am not an eye, I do not belong to the body," it would not for that reason cease to be part of the body. If the whole body were an eye, where would the sense of hearing be? If the whole body were an ear, where would the sense of smell be? But in fact God has arranged the parts in the body, every one of them, just as he wanted them to be. If they were all one part, where would the body be? As it is, there are many parts, but one body." (1 Cor. 12:14-20).

It is so sad that many people value themselves by how they look. I think women are especially critical of themselves. God does not look at the outside, but at the heart. *"Your beauty should not come from outward adornment, such as braided hair and the wearing of gold jewelry and fine clothes. Instead, it should be that of your inner self, the unfading beauty of a gentle and quiet spirit, which is of great worth in God's sight."* (1 Peter 3:3-4).

Maybe you have tried and failed many times, and some people have given up on you. Just remember, God never gives up on you. When Jesus was hanging on the cross with two convicted thieves, one was badgering Jesus, but the second thief said, *"We are punished justly, for we are getting what our deeds deserve. But this man has done nothing wrong."* Then he said, *"Jesus, remember me when you come into your kingdom."* Jesus answered him, *"I tell you the truth, today you will be with me in paradise."* (Luke 23:41-43).

The second thief was remorseful and repented for what he had done in his life. It was not possible for the second thief to perform any good works or even be baptized, but because he repented and asked Jesus to remember him; that thief is in paradise today. Jesus does not want any of us to wait until the end of our life on earth to receive His gift of salvation and a new and better way of living. 2 Corinthians 6:2 reads, *"For God says, "At just the right time, I heard you. On the day of salvation, I helped you. Indeed, the "right time" is now. Today is the day of salvation"* (NLT). Don't delay accepting Jesus as your Savior and Lord of your life; do it right now, if you haven't done it already! If we are to have the best new life possible, we need to study the Bible to learn how God says we should live. We need to have confidence to make changes and live that new life. The Bible has a lot to say about confidence.

"For the LORD will be your confidence and will keep your foot from being snared." (Proverbs 3:26).

The fruit of righteousness will be peace; the effect of righteousness will be quietness and confidence forever." (Isaiah 32:17).

"But blessed is the man who trusts in the LORD, whose confidence is in him." (Jeremiah 17:7).

In him [Jesus] *and through faith in him we may approach God with freedom and confidence."* (Ephesians 3:12).

Let us then approach the throne of grace with confidence, so that we may receive mercy and find grace to help us in our time of need."

(Hebrews 4:16). When you are fighting temptation and struggling to stay on the right path, run to Jesus. He is our mediator and mentor. He understands our struggles and eagerly waits to stand with us and uphold us on those slippery slopes. We have choices. He is always the right one. Don't hesitate; run to Him.

So we say with confidence, "The Lord is my helper; I will not be afraid. What can man do to me?" (Hebrews 13:6).

In this way, love is made complete among us so that we will have confidence on the day of judgment, because in this world we are like him." (1 John 4:17).

This is the confidence we have in approaching God: that if we ask anything according to his will, he hears us." (1 John 5:14).

Our confidence should be in trusting God for His wisdom, accepting that Jesus died for our sins, and the Holy Spirit will guide us if we will listen. Our confidence is not in ourselves, but in Him.

CHAPTER 7
GUILT AND SHAME

When we accept Jesus as our Lord and Savior, we receive all the benefits of being adopted and we have an abundant eternal inheritance awaiting us in heaven; but, what about here and now? You are a child of God! The Bible tells us God is our Abba Father (Daddy). He knows everything about us, and still loves us more than anyone we have ever known.

Because it is impossible for us to completely love unconditionally, we have a hard time accepting unconditional love as even being possible. Probably the closest we can relate to that kind of love would be through a wonderful mother or a loving, faithful dog. How can we be worthy of that kind of love? We are not worthy, but we are made perfect through the death of Jesus that paid for our sins. Jesus paid the highest price possible for us; Himself. Jesus loves each one of us and has promised to always be with us and never leave us.

Because of things we have done in our lives, we do not feel worthy of His love. How can we change the way we see and feel about ourselves to be able to freely accept His love? Think about the person (or even an animal) that you feel loved you the most. When someone truly loves you, they want to see you and spend time with you. Just being able to sit together in the same room with someone you love can make you feel loved, joyful and content. Hebrews 10:22 tells us, *"let us draw near to God with a sincere heart in full assurance of faith, having our hearts sprinkled to cleanse us from a guilty conscience and having our bodies washed with pure water."*

When we feel guilt and shame, we may think that we should just hang our head in shame and hide; but that is not what God instructs us to do. In Hebrews 4:16 we read, *"Let us then approach the throne of grace with confidence, so that we may receive mercy and find grace to help us in our time of need."*

Jesus faced every temptation we have, but He did not sin. He yearns to have us come to Him to be loved, strengthened and forgiven.

The first action we should take is to acknowledge our sin. I know we hate to think about something bad, embarrassing and shameful we have done, but when David did, he found the forgiveness he craved. In Psalm 32:5 it says, *"Then I acknowledged my sin to you and did not cover up my iniquity. I said, "I will confess my transgressions to the Lord—and you forgave the guilt of my sin."*

If we are to live a life pleasing to God, we must face those wrong things we have done. It is when we feel the full weight of what we have done, true repentance can come and we can seek God's strength indwelling us so we do not repeat that harmful and hurtful action. If what we have done is a habit in our lives, we must consider a new and different way to handle our weaknesses. There are many programs out there just waiting to help you start a new life. A program can be very helpful, but it is the power of God through the Holy Spirit in you that will make the difference.

When I was very young, I remember hanging and swinging on the large metal storage cabinet in our kitchen. My parents were in the field planting corn, so I thought I would never be caught and could swing on the dish cupboard. It was about six feet tall and three feet wide and the large metal front door was perfect for little me to swing on. I got more adventurous as time passed and started pushing off harder and faster with each swing back and forth. It wasn't until I noticed the entire cabinet starting to fall forward with all of its contents and me that I knew I was in trouble. Luckily for me, I swung to the side and let loose before the cupboard and all the glass and metal dishes slammed to the kitchen floor.

The sound was so deafening that my parents heard it all the way in the field. My mom and step-dad rushed into the house to find me crying hysterically and the cupboard on the floor surrounded by many broken dishes. I thought I was sure to receive a deserved whipping, but instead my mom hugged me and asked in a panic if I was alright. I told her how I was swinging on the door and the cabinet fell over. I don't think I even got a spanking because my mom was just so glad that I was okay. We were very poor and I knew that we didn't have extra money to replace those broken dishes. My mom had every right to be angry with me.

That was one of the best lessons I ever learned about forgiving people when they make mistakes. My mom said she knew I didn't intentionally pull the cabinet over and break the dishes and she hoped I wouldn't be doing dangerous things like that in the future. I was so thankful that she forgave me that I made a conscious effort to not cause her or my step-dad to worry again.

My sisters did normal teenage rebellious acts growing up, but my mom would've told you that I never gave them a moment's worry. I saw how my sisters staying out past curfew worried my mom and I vowed that I would never do that. I never did anything for which I was grounded. One time my mom told me it was hard for them to sleep when I stayed up late reading because the light shined through their curtains. (The bedroom my sisters and I shared in Alaska was an addition built on to a trailer.) Even though I didn't realize the light would shine into their room, I was so disappointed in myself for not being more considerate that I grounded myself for a week.

When we truly realize how much we love someone, we try to act in a way that is pleasing to them. If we stop to ponder what God did in letting his son die for our sins, and realize the pain and agony that caused; we should be motivated to live our lives in a way that is pleasing to Him. It is far better to say no to our friends request to join them in any activity that might not be God's best for us than to gain their acceptance and disappoint our loving Heavenly Father. Guilt and shame are like a lingering painful boil that torments us and will not heal.

Through the grace and mercy of Jesus, our sins can be blotted out never to haunt us again. When we sin, we can repent and ask for God's forgiveness; and He is faithful to forgive us. Even better than that is when we live our lives as our role model Jesus did. We can be tempted and yet not sin. Pray for help in times of temptation, and the Holy Spirit within you can give you the strength to overcome what is tempting you (1 Corinthians 10:12-13).

Ezekiel 18:20 tells us, ". . . *The righteousness of the righteous man will be credited to him, and the wickedness of the wicked will be charged against him.*" We have the choice; we will reap what we sow. Your Heavenly Father, Jesus and the Holy Spirit are all cheering you on to persevere and do the right thing.

Psalm 34:4-5 tells us, "*I sought the Lord, and he answered me; he delivered me from all my fears. Those who look to him are radiant; their faces are never covered with shame.*" When you have failed, that is the time to realize that God's ways are the right ways. Consider your sins to be life lessons to keep you from following the wrong path in the future.

Every day is a new opportunity to live your life as the loving and grateful child you want to be for God. In Lamentations 3:22-23 we read, "*Because of the Lord's great love we are not consumed, for his compassions never fail. They are new every morning; great is your faithfulness.*" Don't hang your head and dread the day ahead. Look up to see a loving Heavenly Father who created you for good works. It is when we are humble and realize we have so much to be forgiven, that we become moldable clay that God can use.

In Luke 7:47 it says, "*Therefore, I tell you, her many sins have been forgiven—for she loved much. But he who has been forgiven little loves little.*" It was those who thought they were righteous (but were unloving) that Jesus called a brood of vipers.

In Matthew 9:10-13 we read about who Jesus spent his time with. *"While Jesus was having dinner at Matthew's house, many tax collectors and "sinners" came and ate with him and his disciples. When the Pharisees saw this, they asked his disciples, "Why does your teacher eat with tax collectors and 'sinners'? On hearing this, Jesus said, "It is not the healthy who need a doctor, but the sick. But go and learn what this means: 'I desire mercy, not sacrifice.' For I have not come to call the righteous, but sinners."*

Jesus came to live on this earth to be our savior and teach us how to live life. No matter what you have done, God can give you a new life. In Ezekiel 36:26 it says, *"I will give you a new heart and put a new spirit in you; I will remove from you your heart of stone and give you a heart of flesh."* Thank you God!

CHAPTER 8
BEING A GOOD STEWARD OF TIME, ENERGY & MONEY

We know that God created us, and Jesus died for our sins; but how should that change us and how we live our lives? Since God prepared things in advance for us to do, we should find out what those things are. Discover your gifts, and find the place where God wants you to use the gifts He has given you.

The Bible has a great story about talents. The word talent used here was a measurement often used to weigh silver and gold, but it's no coincidence that it also means our God-given talents. A talent in this story was worth more than a thousand dollars.

"To one he gave five talents of money, to another two talents, and to another one talent, each according to his ability. Then he went on his journey. The man who had received the five talents went at once and put his money to work and gained five more. So also, the one with the two talents gained two more. But the man who had received the

one talent went off, dug a hole in the ground and hid his master's money."

"After a long time the master of those servants returned and settled accounts with them. The man who had received the five talents brought the other five. 'Master,' he said, 'you entrusted me with five talents. See, I have gained five more.' "His master replied, 'Well done, good and faithful servant! You have been faithful with a few things; I will put you in charge of many things. Come and share your master's happiness!'

"The man with the two talents also came. 'Master,' he said, 'you entrusted me with two talents; see, I have gained two more.' "His master replied, 'Well done, good and faithful servant! You have been faithful with a few things; I will put you in charge of many things. Come and share your master's happiness!'

"Then the man who had received the one talent came. 'Master,' he said, 'I knew that you are a hard man, harvesting where you have not sown and gathering where you have not scattered seed. So I was afraid and went out and hid your talent in the ground. See, here is what belongs to you.' "His master replied, 'You wicked, lazy servant! So you knew that I harvest where I have not sown and gather where I have not scattered seed? Well then, you should have put my money on deposit with the bankers, so that when I returned I would have received it back with interest. "'Take the talent from him and give it to the one who has the ten talents." (Matthew 25:15-28).

Wow, that seems pretty severe. The story definitely says we should be using the talents God gave us and investing them in others instead of burying them. So what does God say we should be doing with our talents? The verse many people think of as the key is John 3:16. It says, *"For God so loved the world that he gave his one and only Son, that whoever believes in him shall not perish but have eternal life."*

God's priority is to love people and save them through Jesus so we can all be with God, Jesus, and the Holy Spirit for eternity. We really need to have the right attitude to start. Whose attitude should we model? In Philippians 2:5 it says, *"Your attitude should be the same as that of Christ Jesus."*

If we use our God given talents out of love, then we're going in the right direction. Don't think about grueling sacrifice, because Jesus said, *"But go and learn what this means: 'I desire mercy, not sacrifice.' For I have not come to call the righteous, but sinners."* (Matthew 9:13).

The point is not even what we do; it is that whatever we do, we do it with love. Let's look at more verses that tell us what our service to God and others should look like.

"He has showed you, O man, what is good. And what does the Lord require of you? To act justly and to love mercy and to walk humbly with your God." (Micah 6:8).

When Jesus was asked what the most important commandment was, He [Jesus] answered: *"'Love the Lord your God with all your heart and with all your soul and with all your strength and with all your mind'; and, 'Love your neighbor as yourself.'"* (Luke 10:27).

Other verses tell us, *"Be completely humble and gentle; be patient, bearing with one another in love"*. (Ephesians 4:2).

"Therefore, as God's chosen people, holy and dearly loved, clothe yourselves with compassion, kindness, humility, gentleness and patience". (Colossians 3:12).

"If I have the gift of prophecy and can fathom all mysteries and all knowledge, and if I have a faith that can move mountains, but have not love, I am nothing". (1 Corinthians 13:2).

Read that last verse again. It would be amazing to see someone move a mountain, but God tells us that even if we do spectacular things, if we don't do them with love; they will count as nothing. I know some people seem hard to love. It has helped me to pray to God to help me see with His eyes, speak with His heart, and be His hands and feet. Love and compassion given by God can enable you to do things you never thought possible.

When I was criticized by a teacher in second grade for not being able to speak clearly, I was embarrassed and teased by my peers. Even though the teacher apologized after she found out I was born with a tied tongue, the damage was done. I vowed never again to speak in front of people I did not know and trust unless I had to. For the next 27 years, I kept that vow.

I now speak almost weekly at a mission's homeless shelter for women and children. How did that change come about? God began to open my heart and spirit to see the pain and hurt in other people. I had been quietly serving in the background. My best friend suggested that the church was encouraging women who felt led to go to the School of Women's Ministry training. Three of us of traveled back and forth for over a year. We graduated in March 2006.

In our training we learned that whatever we had gone through, there would be someone that had either gone through it, was currently going through it, or would be going through it in the future. The speaker told us that if we truly wanted to love people, we also had to share ourselves.

We had to do a project to receive credit for graduation. After taking a Spiritual Gifts Assessment Test, I knew my strongest gift was encouragement. (There are many resources available by book or on the internet to help you discover your own spiritual gifts God has given you). I knew that I received so much encouragement every year from attending the Women of Faith conferences. I called and asked if I could use the DVDs I had purchased to show at the shelter for the women. Women of Faith not only gave their permission, but also their blessing.

I went for six weeks and spoke after the videos about how we could use what we had learned in the videos in our lives. I also chose four to six songs to sing that repeated the lesson we had heard. At the end of the six weeks I was in love with the ladies and have never stopped going.

I have spoken at three women's retreats, but those were harder for me. It was hard for me to share my failures and sins with women I was not sure shared my struggles. The first time as I was preparing, I thought I knew exactly what I should say. The Holy Spirit kept gently telling me I was to tell them about my depression and suicidal feelings when I was bedridden for a year with little chance for improvement. Every time I sat down at the computer to type, the system would crash. I finally got the message and started writing about my feelings of doubt and desperation, but wondering all the time why I should talk about that. I prayed that God would sometime in the future let me know why I had to talk about such a depressing topic.

I was shaking, sweaty and teary-eyed as I spoke about my feelings of worthlessness and thinking my family would be so much better off without me. God used those months to teach me that my worth was not in what I could accomplish physically, but that I was there to love them, hug them and listen to them.

The very next morning as I was coming down the stairs, a young woman asked if I would come into her room to talk with her. I went in and she shared that the past year had been a terrible struggle and that she felt like such a failure with her family and her job. She said she told God if something didn't happen that weekend, when she returned home she was going to kill herself. She told me that what I said was exactly what she needed to hear. Wow, God is so loving and caring. Through my story, God had given her hope. Any feelings of fear or judgment I was afraid to suffer quickly vanished as I thanked God for allowing me to help that dear lady.

Am I still nervous when I speak? Yes, usually; but each time it seems a little easier. There have been times at the shelter when women have yelled at me or heckled me. In their pain, they did not believe that God sees us and cares. It is especially for those women that I continue to go. Throughout time God has now matured my gifts to include teaching and service. When you begin to love others passionately, you realize what a privilege it is to share our loving and merciful God with those who do not know Him.

Another pain that people struggle with is the loss of a loved one. Why God takes someone we love so much and before we think it should be their time is hard to accept. The story of losing our second daughter is included in Chapter 1—Miracles from God. I am careful to share this every year so the ladies in the program hear it at least once before they graduate. Some people ask why I would choose to relive that pain and loss, but they need to hear the blessings that came through that tragedy. Romans 8:28 tells us, *"And we know that in all things God works for the good of those who love him, who have been called according to His purpose."*

It was probably only the second time I had shared the story of losing our second daughter when I noticed a lady in the back of the room who looked very sad, lonely and not very friendly. At the end of chapel she came forward and asked if she could hold the porcelain painted picture of our daughter. I said of course, and handed it to her. She looked at our beautiful little girl and tears streamed down her cheeks. She handed the plaque back to me and left.

When I had completed gathering all of my things and left the shelter, that lady was waiting for me outside. She told me she had gotten pregnant at 17 and her boyfriend deserted her and she was ashamed to tell her family. She got an abortion and had felt the pain and loss everyday since. Later when she tried to have children, she was never able to conceive. She said she had never stopped to consider that God loved her baby and immediately the baby was carried into heaven. She doesn't even know if her baby is a boy or girl, but she has the assurance that her baby is in heaven and will rejoice when her Mommy comes to heaven to be with her.

The woman told me hearing that her child was in heaven and that she could join her at the end of her life was the first joy she had felt in years. I am so thankful God gave me the courage to overcome my fear of speaking so I can share what a loving, faithful, and forgiving Savior we have. Please don't miss out on using your gifts to encourage others in their time of pain and sorrow.

The Bible tells us, *"Rejoice with those who rejoice; mourn with those who mourn."*(Romans 12:15). Share yourself with others. It divides the pain and multiplies the joy. When you invest your time, energy and money in God's kingdom work, the rewards are eternal!

The Bible tells us in Hebrews 10:24-25, *"And let us consider how we may spur one another on toward love and good deeds. Let us not give up meeting together, as some are in the habit of doing, but let us encourage one another—and all the more as you see the Day approaching."*

The Bible says that iron sharpens iron, and if we are to grow as Christians, we need to be around other Christians who are growing. When we study together, we gain insight from others that we might have missed on our own.

In California, where I live, I see so many people who are never content with what they have. I have 3 favorite verses that talk about contentment. *"I know what it is to be in need, and I know what it is to have plenty. I have learned the secret of being content in any and every situation, whether well fed or hungry, whether living in plenty or in want."* (Philippians 4:12).

"But godliness with contentment is great gain". (1 Timothy 6:6).

By far the best nugget of wisdom is, *"Keep your lives free from the love of money and be content with what you have, because God has said, "Never will I leave you; never will I forsake you."* (Hebrews 13:5).

I am fortunate to have been raised monetarily poor, because I know there is a big difference between needs and wants. When we are good stewards of the assets God has blessed us with (time, energy and money), we can have some left over with which we can bless others. As children of God we need to not only live within our means, but below our means, so we have funds to use for heavenly purposes.

Let me share some examples with you of how to have money left over at the end of the month. When I was still working, I was sharing with a co-worker that we were preparing to go on vacation. She told me she had not been able to go on a vacation in years.

I noticed that she bought a soda from the vending machine everyday. At that time, she was paying $1.00 everyday, 5 days a week, for 49 weeks (minus 3 weeks vacation) a year. I can buy my diet generic soda for $2.60 for a 12-pack, including CRV (California Redemption Value). My sodas were costing me 22 cents a day. I saved 78 cents every day. That saved $3.90 per week. Every year I saved $191.10 minimum. Both my husband and I worked 34 years and both carried our lunches. The $191.10 times 2 times 34 equals $12,994.80 saved during our working careers. That would pay for a lot of vacations and charitable donations.

Another way to save is by buying the store's own generic brand products instead of the name brand. We used to buy name brand frozen mixed vegetables instead of the generic brand. The generic brand included lima beans which my husband did not like. I don't mind them, so I just take all of those. The difference when I shopped this week is only 20 cents, but what is the compounding affect? Those 20 cents per week times 52 weeks times 40 years equals $416.00. For that amount, I don't mind eating lima beans.

Many people spend everything they make. Some people believe that God will provide everything as they need it. God also tells us to be wise. We should plan for the inevitable repair and replacement of tires, appliances and clothing. In Proverbs 6:6-8 we read, *"Go to the ant, you sluggard; consider its ways and be wise! It has no commander, no overseer or ruler, yet it stores its provisions in summer and gathers its food at harvest."*

Remember the story in Genesis about Joseph. It was only because Joseph saved food during the seven years of great abundance that Egypt had the resources to survive during the seven years of famine. Saving is good but not if you do it to accrue dollar signs in a bank account and don't use it to supply goods and services as they are needed.

In Bible Study Fellowship we heard a story about a very wealthy woman who would not spend her money. Her name was Hetty Green (1834-1916). "Estimates of her net worth ranged from $100 million to $200 million (or $1.9—$3.8 billion in 2006 dollars), arguably making her the richest woman in the world at the time." "In her old age, Hetty Green began to suffer from a bad hernia, but refused to have an operation because it cost $150." Her son also had to have his leg amputated due in part to her delaying to seek proper medical care.

Small amounts compound to become large amounts. Jesus' parable about stewardship from Luke 19 says, *"Well done, my good servant!' his master replied. 'Because you have been trustworthy in a very small matter, take charge of ten cities."* (Luke 19:17). Being conscientious about how you spend your time, energy and money can make a big difference in your life and the lives of others.

I have a few television programs I enjoy, but I was getting to bed too late after watching them. After reading about ways to save time, I realized if I used every commercial to prepare for bed, I could hit the hay as soon as the show ended. That small act gave me approximately 15 more minutes of precious sleep every night. By the end of the week, I had accrued over an hour of additional sleep.

When I thought about how I was spending my free time, I found some of it was spent mindlessly watching television programs that I didn't really enjoy (especially those reality TV shows). I now consciously watch only news, and family friendly shows. The extra time I have carved out is now spent reading inspiring stories or downloading inspirational music for us to sing at the mission. In 1 Timothy 4:7-8 we are instructed, *"Have nothing to do with godless myths and old wives' tales; rather, train yourself to be godly. For physical training is of some value, but godliness has value for all things, holding promise for both the present life and the life to come."*

My dreaded chore is now done first and then the rest of my day can be spent doing things that are more enjoyable and without that lingering dread of the chore I was avoiding. When you have a big chore, break it down into bite-sized pieces. Cleaning that refrigerator can be done one shelf or drawer at a time.

I don't have an endless abundance of energy, but there is so much I want to do. When you are tired, taking the extra effort to exercise and eat nutritious foods is hard; however, when you make those choices to add proper nutrition and exercise, you will have more energy. One example that really shows the wisdom of considering what you put into yourself for energy is the folly there would be to put sugar into your beautiful car's gas tank. That sugar is not going to get that car anywhere. The same is true for your body.

I became diabetic 4 years ago, so I had to rethink what I ate, how much, and how often. I started eating 3 small meals a day plus 3 healthy snacks in between. I also stretch every morning and walk 3 to 5 times a week. In the past 2 years I have lost 15 pounds and am now at my ideal weight. I know 15 pounds doesn't sound like a lot, but the knee I injured years ago cross-county skiing that used to bother me almost daily, seldom bothers me anymore.

I thought eating more often would make me gain weight, but the smaller portions and eating more consistently has increased my metabolism. There are definitely times I miss my nightly desserts, but I enjoy my increased energy and better health more than I miss my sugar-laden delights. I do treat myself with more healthy and nutritious goodies so I don't feel deprived and become cranky.

Life should always be kept in balance. If you wait to schedule family fun time until everything is done, you will seldom find time to enjoy yourself. All work and no play do make Jack a dull, cranky, and testy boy. Set aside time to spend with your spouse, family and friends. Jesus could have spent his entire short life healing people, but he knew he also needed time with God and time with his friends.

We can become so heavenly minded that we are no earthly good. The Thessalonians needed to be reminded that even though Jesus was coming again, they needed to work so they were not a burden on others. Ecclesiastes tells us that there is a time for every season. Be sure to keep balance in your life. We should love God, our families, other people; and don't forget to care for yourself also. Take good care of yourself, you belong to God.

Try to consciously have an attitude of gratitude. When it comes to your attitude, you can be a stressor or a blesser. If whatever you do, you do with love, you will be a blesser.

CHAPTER 9
FEAR

One of my favorite verses that I always think of when I start to feel fearful is 2 Timothy 1:7. I will share 2 versions of it. The first verse reads, *"For God has not given us a spirit of fear, but of power and of love and of a sound mind."* (NKJV). The New International Version reads, *"For God did not give us a spirit of timidity, but a spirit of power, of love and of self-discipline."*

It is important when we start to be fearful to remember the words Paul used to encourage the first Christians, *"What, then, shall we say in response to this (those who love God)? If God is for us, who can be against us?"* (Romans 8:31). During times of danger, worry, or anxiety, remember God is with us if we have accepted Him as Savior and Lord of our lives.

When our daughter was preparing to go away to college, I became anxious. All of the areas where her chosen universities were located were in relatively large cities. I was worried about the crime and people harming her. Cutting those apron strings to allow our children to fly on their own is so hard to do; yet that is our job as parents. We can't always be there to watch over them. We are to raise our children to seek God in their lives, mature in their character, education, and skills and be able to be independent. We need to allow them to spread their wings and fly in ever widening circles.

The winter before our daughter was to go away, I had taken our car in to have some work done. When I was dropped off to pick it up, it wasn't ready. The dealership drove me a block away to a rental car company. After I had signed the paperwork, I left the building to get in the rental car. There was a delay as I searched in the near darkness to find the seat changing mechanism and the ignition. I heard a man speaking loudly in my direction and soon realized he was speaking to me. He was saying, "I have a gun, get out of the car, I'm going to shoot you." I even remember thinking, why should I get out of the car so you can shoot me. I couldn't believe what I was hearing. I looked in the field just below the parking lot, and there were four men and one was pointing a large handgun at me.

I knew that a television show I had seen said you should throw the keys one way and run the other; but I had a terrible feeling that I did not want to be taken by those men. The man's voice which had started strong and firm began to be louder and contain many expletives. I had no qualms about handing over the rental car, but I did not want to hand myself over to them. I decided that if it was my day to die, it would be right then and not after going with those angry men.

The parking lot was on a raised retaining wall about four feet above the field. I was hoping that if he shot, it would ricochet off the engine. I had ducked my head between my knees all the while searching for the horn or ignition with my hands.

The man had become very violent and menacing in his speech. I said a quick prayer thanking God that I knew I would be alright if I died, but I asked that He would be with my daughter and husband if I was taken from them. Immediately I felt a sense of peace. Soon after that, it got strangely quiet and a few moments later there was a knock on my side window. I looked up and saw the two men from the rental company.

One of them asked me if I was okay. I said, "I don't know. What was that man saying to me?" He said, "The man was yelling at you, 'I have a gun, get out of the car or I'm going to shoot you.'" I missed hearing that one tiny word "or", but I don't think it would have made any difference. I was told as the two men came out of the business, they saw the four men running across the field where a fifth man was waiting for them.

I was so relieved and shaken that I told the rental car men I was okay, and I drove away. All I wanted was to go home to my family and lock the door. I was going to stop at a fast food restaurant to get supper, but I didn't want to get out of the car so I went to a drive through instead.

The next day when I told my co-workers about it, they said I should call the police. I am normally a very conscientious citizen, but after that intimidating experience, staying at that place any longer was not on my list of things to do. When I called the police station, the woman answering the phone jumped all over me for not calling at the time it happened. Thank goodness the officer who came and took my report was more compassionate. He said my actions might not seem like the best choice, but because I survived, my choice was probably fine.

The officer told me another car was stolen two blocks away from where my attempted carjacking occurred and used as a getaway car to rob a Montgomery Wards store. One of the men had smashed a jewelry case and cut himself while grabbing through the broken case. The DNA that was gathered from the blood linked the men to the case. They were bad men who had rap sheets a mile long. I couldn't believe our town had bad men like that.

I had already made plans to go on a moonlight cross-country ski trip with two of my girlfriends two days later. I love the beauty of snow in the forest, but it was a little eerie. My parents had always taught us that if you fall off a horse, you get right back on. I knew I did not want fear to control my life. I did take a self-defense course and I am more careful now, but I don't want fear to keep me from enjoying the beautiful, exciting adventures that God has for us to enjoy.

Sometimes we fear things with which we are not familiar. Cities have always been intimidating to me. When I thought about small towns being safer, I remembered the real tragedy that occurred in Manley Hot Springs, Alaska. It was a small town with a natural hot springs that I had visited as a child with my family. In 1984 a drifter killed 9 people in that small fishing village that only had a population of 80. Sin is everywhere.

The Bible tells us, *"I am sending you out like sheep among wolves. Therefore be as shrewd as snakes and as innocent as doves."* If you are a child of God and become fearful, remember, *"You, dear children, are from God and have overcome them, because the one who is in you is greater than the one who is in the world."*

When I had the opportunity to go to Israel for a tour in 2010, I was ecstatic. Some family members and friends were hesitant for me to go because of the unrest which has lingered there since Biblical times. There were forty-two of us from five different churches, and I don't think any of us were fearful. We were all so excited to see all those places we had read about in the Bible and to walk where Jesus walked. We did heed the warning of the tour company and did not go to Bethlehem.

I had such a passion to go to Israel and I knew that the worst that could happen would be if we were killed. As a Christian, I know when I die, I will be with Jesus in heaven. I love the way The Message puts it in 2 Corinthians 5:6-8, *"That's why we live with such good cheer. You won't see us drooping our heads or dragging our feet! Cramped conditions here don't get us down. They only remind us of the spacious living conditions ahead. It's what we trust in but don't yet see that keeps us going. Do you suppose a few ruts in the road or rocks in the path are going to stop us? When the time comes, we'll be plenty ready to exchange exile for homecoming."* Amen.

CHAPTER 10
RELATIONSHIPS

With our hectic lifestyles it is hard to maintain good relationships. Even Jesus became frustrated when his friends failed to "be there" for him. In Matthew we read that Jesus went to the garden of Gethsemane to pray. He said to his friends, *"My soul is overwhelmed with sorrow to the point of death. Stay here and keep watch with me."*

After praying, Jesus returned to his friends and found them sleeping. *"Could you men not keep watch with me for one hour?"* *he asked Peter.*

Even though Jesus was disappointed with his friends, he did not cut them off or hold a grudge. Even when Peter had denied knowing Jesus three times after Jesus had been arrested, Jesus did not give up on Peter.

Remember in Matthew that Peter was originally called Simon. Peter had shown so much promise. When Jesus had asked him, *"Who do you say I am?"* *Simon answered, "You are the Christ, the*

Son of the living God." Jesus replied, "Blessed are you, Simon son of Jonah, for this was not revealed to you by man, but by my Father in heaven. And I tell you that you are Peter [meaning "stone"], and on this rock I will build my church, and the gates of Hades will not overcome it. I will give you the keys of the kingdom of heaven; whatever you bind on earth will be bound in heaven, and whatever you loose on earth will be loosed in heaven."

After such glowing praise and encouragement from Jesus, you would think that would have cemented their relationship. Admit it; we all have those weak moments when we don't live up to people's expectations or even our own. Jesus knew the heart of Peter, and Peter became not just an apostle of Jesus, but he later wrote immensely wise and loving words to help us live lives pleasing to God. Peter had denied Jesus three times before the rooster crowed, but Peter went on to serve well and because of Peter's boldness and courage, he was later martyred during Nero's reign.

If you have failed and need to get up and try again, you are in good company. When we stop to realize all that we have done wrong, we should have a deep gratitude and humbleness that can make us even better servants for God.

When I think about the people that are my best friends, all of them are good listeners that speak the truth in love. Proverbs 15:4 tells us, *"The tongue that brings healing is a tree of life, but a deceitful tongue crushes the spirit."* God wants us to lift each other up, not tear each other down.

In Luke chapter 7 Jesus speaks lovingly about a sinful woman who came and washed His feet with her tears and wiped them with her hair. One of the Pharisee's who was there was disgusted that Jesus allowed her to even touch Him. Jesus said to the Pharisee, *"Therefore, I tell you, her many sins have been forgiven-for she loved much. But he who has been forgiven little loves little."*

When I was a teenager, I was probably closer to being a Pharisee than a saint. I tried to follow every commandment and law and was very self-controlled. Somehow I thought that made me better than some people. What I have learned is that my heart was hardened against people I thought were not doing the right things. I am so thankful that God allowed me to live in Korea for a year where life was so different than what I had experienced in the United States.

When I left Tucson it had been warm and about 75 degrees. When I reached Osan, Korea, it was below zero. Within two weeks I had acute bronchitis. I had gotten very sick and knew I was going to lose consciousness. My husband was at work on the base, so I went and knocked on the neighbor's door. As I introduced myself to the GI and his Korean girlfriend, I fainted.

The nice young man had his girlfriend hail a cab and he took me onto the base. I was given a shot and some antibiotics and my husband was contacted. For the next few days the girl next door, I'll call her Yun, brought me food and cared for me. I was scared and depressed. It was my first time in a foreign country and I didn't know anyone except my husband and I did not speak any Korean. Yun was so gracious and kind to me.

Through the next few days I learned that Yun had come from a very poor family. Her parents were older and were unable to earn much money. Yun had started cleaning for a mama-san (a woman in charge of the young girls at a bar or brothel). The mama-san had urged Yun to borrow money to care for her parents.

Before very long Yun had accrued a large debt and the mama-san said Yun would have to become a bar girl or she would have her thrown in jail. Yun tried to keep that information from her parents, but they found out. Her family threw Yun out of their house and disowned her. She had done the only thing she knew to care for her family, but now she had no family and no way to pay the debt that the mama-san required. She was a warm and caring young woman who was tricked into servitude.

She was required to do anything and everything the men wanted, and the largest part of the money went back to the mama-san. It took a long time for Yun to buy her freedom, but by then she thought being a bar girl was the only job available to her. Her beauty and kindness were evident to everyone, so often she would be a yobo (Korean rent-a-wife or mistress) to one GI for the length of his stay in Korea.

A few months after Yun had cared for me, she had to have some female surgery due to an implanted birth control device. I was able to care for her and there was a deep bond between us. A few years later an American man proposed to her and she moved to the United States. If there was ever a woman who deserved a better life, it was Yun.

I am so thankful to have met Yun because I learned to never judge another person. We have no way of knowing exactly what they have been through in life and what they have had to do to survive. It is God's job to judge and it is our job to love. God sees their hearts and knows their intentions.

Probably the hardest relationship is marriage. After you live with someone for a long time, you often take each other for granted and don't use the self-control and respect you give to others. There are many books and seminars that have helped me immensely in learning to accept the differences that cause antagonism between us due to our gender, priorities and how we were raised. I love the video series called, "Love & Respect" by Dr. Emerson and Sarah Eggerichs. There is also a book by that title.

Men and women don't choose to be hard to understand; we are just different. Life is a lot easier if you just accept that fact. Men and women often don't respond the same way because we are created to be different by God. Men are usually physically stronger and diagnose situations by facts. Women are usually physically weaker and driven by emotions and maternal instincts. It was never intended for us to be alike, or one of us wouldn't be needed. We are like puzzle pieces which need to be opposite of each other to fill in each other's blank spots.

Our best relationships will usually be with people who have the same motivation and priorities that we have. If one person is a passionate Christian and the other lives for parties and pleasing their own desires, there is no solid common base to strengthen that relationship.

God tells us, "*Do not be yoked together with unbelievers. For what do righteousness and wickedness have in common? Or what fellowship can light have with darkness?*" (2 Corinthians 6:14).

As Christians, we should daily study the Bible, weekly attend church and also belong to a group of believers who are trying to grow and mature in their Christian walk. When we have Christ as our solid foundation, we can then spend time with our unsaved peers. When our convictions and faith are strong enough not to waiver in the face of peer pressure, we can then be salt and light to those who have not accepted Jesus Christ as their Savior and Lord of their lives.

Usually most people do not care about what we know until they know that we care. Very often you will not be able to speak into someone's life until you have a relationship with them. When you ask God to teach you to see other people as He sees them, it will amaze you how much love and compassion you will begin to have for others.

Jesus spent time with tax collectors and sinners. When the Pharisees criticized Him for this, Jesus' response was, *"It is not the healthy who need a doctor, but the sick. But go and learn what this means: 'I desire mercy, not sacrifice.' For I have not come to call the righteous, but sinners."* (Matthew 9:12-13).

In *The Standard Encyclopedic Dictionary*, mercy is described as, "Kind or compassionate treatment of an offender, adversary, prisoner, etc., in one's power. A disposition to be kind, forgiving, or helpful." Sacrifice is described as, "The act of making an offering to a deity, in worship or atonement; also, that which is so offered. A giving up of some cherished or desired object, person, idea, etc., usually for the sake of something else; also, that which is so given up."

Doesn't it sound like Jesus is telling us that it is even more important to Him that we have compassion for others than to offer things to Him? How are people supposed to hear about Jesus if not from us? In earlier generations, many of the social opportunities were church gatherings. Now, with our 24/7 hectic lives, many people no longer attend a church.

Even though Jesus said He desires mercy and not sacrifice, it is still important that we tithe (give the first 10% of our earnings to God's work). Jesus told the seventy-two he sent out ahead of him, *"Stay in that house, eating and drinking whatever they give you, for the worker deserves his wages. Do not move around from house to house."* (Luke 10:7).

In order for a church to mature in their walk, they need to have a Bible teaching pastor and a place to gather. When you give to a Biblically motivated church and the work of God, you are giving to God. When we support our church, we should also remember to be supportive of those who are in leadership. In 1 Timothy 5:17 it says, *"The elders who direct the affairs of the church well are worthy of double honor, especially those whose work is preaching and teaching."* Hebrews 13:17 tells us, *"Obey your leaders and submit to their authority. They keep watch over you as men who must give an account. Obey them so that their work will be a joy, not a burden, for that would be of no advantage to you."* There cannot be unity in the church if we are tearing each other down. We can hold each other accountable and speak the truth in love without becoming divisive.

It is especially important how we treat our Christian brothers and sisters. Our time spent with others from the body of Christ should be a taste of what heaven will be like. There should be love, respect and unity. In Ephesians 4:2-3 we read, *"Be completely humble and gentle; be patient, bearing with one another in love. Make every effort to keep the unity of the Spirit through the bond of peace."*

Did you notice it doesn't say to just give it a good try; it says to "make every effort". In *The Standard Encyclopedic Dictionary* the description of effort is: "Expenditure of physical, mechanical, or mental energy to get something done; exertion." It is not unusual to see people making little or no effort to get along. In Romans 12:18 it tells us, *"If it is possible, as far as it depends on you, live at peace with everyone."*

If you have done your best, and there is still hostility in a relationship; it may be time for a cooling down period. Sometimes writing a letter is better than a face-to-face encounter. When emotions are strained, sometimes we are so busy thinking of what we are going to say, that we fail to fully listen. The benefits of a letter are that we can complete what we need to say without interruption. We have the time to pray and re-read it many times to be sure we are speaking the truth in love.

If we spent more time commending what someone is doing right, there would probably be a lot more positive interaction and a lot less negative. Never miss the opportunity to thank and encourage those around you.

When James was instructing the early Christians in how they should act toward one another he said, *"If you really keep the royal law found in Scripture, 'Love your neighbor as yourself', you are doing right."* (James 2:8). When you truly care about having a good relationship with others, remember to love them.

The verse above was included in a section of James that spoke about forbidding favoritism. Some people have the mistaken impression that they only need to make an effort to be considerate of select family and friends. James chapter 2 talks about the bias we can sometimes fall into of treating some people better than others. Two of the main points are that we are not to judge others and we are to show mercy to them. James 2:12-13 reads, *"Speak and act as those who are going to be judged by the law that gives freedom, because judgment without mercy will be shown to anyone who has not been merciful. Mercy triumphs over judgment!"*

Another verse that talks about how we are to interact with each other is from Philippians 2:14-15. It says, *"Do everything without complaining or arguing, so that you may become blameless and pure, children of God without fault in a crooked and depraved generation, in which you shine like stars in the universe."* To be that kind of light to those around you is better than any Hollywood star that ever lived.

Jesus said in Matthew 5:9, *"Blessed are the peacemakers, for they will be called sons of God."* What a wonderful compliment to those who work to promote peace. God sees and cares about how we treat each other.

Another standard to consider comes from Philippians 2:3 when it says, *"Do nothing out of selfish ambition or vain conceit, but in humility consider others better than yourselves."* I learned a song that is sung to the tune of Jingle Bells. The song says, "J-O-Y, J-O-Y, this is what joy means; Jesus first and yourself last, and others in-between." When we are led by the heart of Jesus and loving others, life can have great meaning. We can truly be the hands and feet of Jesus.

When we consider others better than ourselves, we won't be as hesitant to lend our time and effort to serve others in whatever way is needed. One thing you have to remember is to love yourself, too. If you exhaust yourself doing for others and don't care for your own nutrition and sleep needs; pretty soon you run out of health and the ability to do for others.

Probably one of the worst mistakes we see is how divorced parents treat each other. Life is hard, but it makes it a lot easier when we can be loved by both a mom and a dad. Once you have children together, you are forever linked and should find a way to be kind and considerate to each other. There was a time that you loved each other, and respect and consideration should continue after the divorce. Not one of us is perfect and the Bible teaches that we will not be forgiven if we do not forgive. When children see parents who cannot be civil to each other, they are being taught that when relationships and situations go bad, you just give up. That can follow all aspects of life including the inability to keep a job. Galatians 6:9 tells us, "*Let us not become weary in doing good, for at the proper time we will reap a harvest if we do not give up.*"

CHAPTER 11
HEALTH, ILLNESS & PAIN

Life is so much easier when we are healthy and energetic. Can you remember a time when you seemed to have limitless energy? No problem seemed too big; but, what about when your body can't keep up with your goals and desires? How can you live an abundant life? It is so easy to get down on yourself and down on life. Peter wrote in 2 Peter 3:1 to encourage Christ's followers to daily live a life pleasing to God. Peter writes, *"Dear friends, this is now my second letter to you. I have written both of them as reminders to stimulate you to wholesome thinking."*

When we dwell on negative thoughts, we are bound to create a negative outlook and a negative attitude. An attitude adjustment is just what the doctor ordered.

Think about Paul being in prison and yet singing and praising God and writing to encourage others. We too serve Jesus, the same Savior and Lord. Only Jesus can put a song in our heart when we are heavy-hearted. How do we turn around our negative thinking? Paul tells us, *"Finally, brothers, whatever is true, whatever is noble, whatever is right, whatever is pure, whatever is lovely, whatever is admirable—if anything is excellent or praiseworthy—think about such things."* (Philippians 4:8).

I have fibromyalgia and osteoarthritis, so it is not unusual for me to have some level of pain. I have learned to think about those things that are working well. I can still stand, walk, see, talk, smell and read. Just counting the blessings we do have makes life seem better. I have read books to learn what to do to best keep my body moving. I often wake up feeling like the tin man. I think if I stay still too long, I will rust in place. I do 20 to 30 minutes of stretching almost every morning. It is not what I really feel like doing, but I know it is best for me. I believe in positive reinforcement, so I don't allow myself to have my big mug of tea in the morning until I have completed my stretching. That is great motivation for me.

To be fit for the Master's work, it takes work. We need to work on our spiritual strength by having time with God and reading His owner's manual for us; the Bible. We need to work on our physical strength so we have the health and energy to be His hands and feet in a hurting world.

When you have fibromyalgia, a small amount of pressure can cause such a large amount of pain. In studying pain, I realize that it was intended to be a warning to us. Without a sense of pain, we would fail to remove our hands when there's too much heat from a flame. It is when leprosy causes skin anesthesia that a leper can lose parts of their extremities. In *Taber's Cyclopedic Medical Dictionary*, it even notes that "rats have been able to remove digits while the patient sleeps." What a blessing to have that pain, that warning to deal with a problem we wouldn't have known otherwise.

I have read books that help me to understand that my pain is not anything compared to what so many have gone through. If you ever think you have it rough, just read *The Hiding Place* by Corrie Ten Boom, *Tortured for Christ* by Pastor Richard Wurmbrand, or *The Heavenly Man* by Brother Yun with Paul Hattaway. I don't ignore my pain if there is something I can do to alleviate it. I take my calcium, vitamin D and Fosamax. I try to concentrate on doing what I can while I can. No one knows what tomorrow will bring, but it is likely my physical health will not improve, so I focus on what I want to do that requires physical stamina.

I am blessed to have completed twenty years of employment with my last employer and have sufficient income and savings to do those things which I have longed to do if I am a good steward of those funds.

Last year I got to go to Zambia, Africa with my friend Barbara to love the children and people there, to speak words of encouragement, and teach some of the wonderful lessons God has taught me.

Last February I had the opportunity to go to Nicaragua and love children that were going to be having surgery themselves or wait while a member of their family had surgery. I got to be part of a medical team and share the love and encouragement that God gives each one of us. Another team member and I got to speak to people there who were attending a program of recovery from alcohol and drugs. My words to them were the same as my words to you. God loves you! You are a wonderful creation of God, you are so loved; and God has a plan and a purpose for your life.

I am fortunate that my spiritual gifts can continue to be used even as my physical body declines. I can encourage, teach and serve every week at the homeless shelter. I can love, listen and hug.

With each tragedy or triumph that comes into our lives, God can use them to mold us into better tools or more useful vessels. I became diabetic four years ago. I have always enjoyed desserts and almost every evening we enjoyed cake, pie or ice cream. We are fortunate to have lived a fairly active lifestyle, and I never carried too much excess weight, but there was a little.

I love learning, but a new way of eating was not something I was happy about. In fact, my pity party that should have stopped shortly after the initial diagnosis, extended for months. I am thankful that my insurance covered a diabetes awareness class with a nurse and dietician.

Whatever your illness, you should find out as much as you can. More knowledge is greater power to control your life and health. We need to realize how severe our illness will be if we don't do what is best for us. I remember the ladies teaching us that if our blood sugar got too high, we could go into a coma and die. If our blood sugar got too low, we could go into a coma and die. Boy, I was depressed, angry and frustrated. I had none of the classic precursors, so it just didn't seem fair that I should have diabetes.

Other than our evening desserts, I had always eaten fairly healthy. It surprised me that I didn't have to deprive myself of all goodies, but I certainly had to learn portion control. We as Americans have learned to super-size everything, and we don't truly have an understanding of what one portion should look like.

In the first two years of eating with my new guidelines, I lost fifteen pounds without trying. Fifteen pounds does not sound like much, but just getting back to my ideal weight has helped my one weak knee to seldom bother me. I now feel healthier and have more energy with my new healthier eating. Romans 8:28 says that God will use all things to our benefit, and He does.

One of the women I regard most highly is Joni Eareckson Tada. At the age of 17, Joni became a quadriplegic after a diving accident. I used to listen to her on the radio every morning as I drove to work. Not only is she an inspiring speaker, but she helped create Wheels for the World and Family Retreats for those that have family members with disabilities. She had a passion, and she found a way to serve those areas that were lacking. She does as much as she can to help those who help her. She does what is required to maintain her health and capabilities. Go to joniandfriends.org to learn more about this remarkable woman.

I have given a lot of thought about how I can live so that I can function as well as possible for as long as possible. Because of problems with circulation, without proper care, amputations can become necessary. I always try to have a plan for any goal I want to attain. Part of planning for illness is to realize there may be a time when you will require the help of others. I have had some family and friends that were in the health care field. I know that a lot of the injuries that health care givers sustain are when they are trying to lift or move patients. I believe it is our responsibility to maintain a healthy weight not only for ourselves, but also to assist those who may have to assist us. It is much easier for me to turn down a second serving of my favorite dish when I relate it to doing it for my family and friends.

When you are struggling with any issue in your life, it is often helpful to talk to others with the same struggle you have. Another one of the remarkable ladies that I have tried to model my outlook after is Barbara Johnson. She was one of the original Women of Faith speakers, and she was such an encouragement to me. When she was diagnosed with diabetes, she asked the doctor to tell her something good about it. The doctor thought for a while and then said, "Well, knowing you, you'll think this is something good. One good thing about having diabetes is that you won't end up in a rest home because usually diabetics don't LIVE that long!" "Oh, that's terrific news!" Barbara said. "Who wants to end up in a rest home anyway?"

I can identify with that. In the last few months of my beloved mother's life, she was not able to walk or even stand by herself. She had always been a doer, but after my step-dad died, she just kind of gave up. Having been bedridden for a year when I was 34, my greatest concern is being a burden on my family. I will do my best to try to be as self-sufficient as possible. I don't really worry about how long I will live, but how well I can give to others while I live. I know God does not care nearly as much about what we accomplish, but that whatever we do, we do with love. I know God values us even when we can accomplish nothing; but we can love others until our last breath.

The next few paragraphs are about learning to take care of ourselves to help us be better able to serve. Please realize that God loves you just the way you are, but we can live wisely and make good choices. Our main aim should be to love God and love others, so please remember: ". . . train yourself to be godly. For physical training is of some value, but godliness has value for all things, holding promise for both the present life and the life to come." (1 Timothy 4:7-8). Loving God and people should always be our first priority.

In Leviticus 19:28 we are told, *"Do not cut your bodies for the dead or put tattoo marks on yourselves. I am the Lord."* There is a note in the NIV Study Bible regarding that verse. The note says, "There was to be no disfiguring of the body, after the manner of the pagans." I thought 'cutting' was a relatively new phenomena; however, Ecclesiastes 1:9 says, *"What has been will be again, what has been done will be done again; there is nothing new under the sun."* I was surprised that in Zambia there is also the problem of cutting and self-injury. The main purpose there seemed to be for self-punishment. Other reasons for cutting are to express and deal with distress and emotional pain. (For more information on this topic, please read the article "Cutting and Self-Harm" at (www.helpguide.org/mental/self_injury.htm). ©Helpguide.org All rights reserved. Visit WWW.HELPGUIDE.ORG for more information and related articles). Wounds in Zambia pose even more of a health problem due to the lack of hygiene and health care. When we injure ourselves, we are weakening our bodies and making it harder for them to be strong and function with their full potential.

There are 3 verses in the New Testament that state we are not under the Old Testament law (Romans 10:4, Galatians 3:23-25, and Ephesians 2:15); however, I believe we should still use wise counsel before we do anything to our bodies. As a mom, my maternal instincts motivate me to share the lessons I have learned in life. Due to having a weakened immune system, I have had to learn to actively seek out ways to regain and maintain my health. Please allow me to share with you some of the points to consider before you get a tattoo. Many problems can result from tattooing. Because the skin is being broken, and a foreign substance is injected into the body, several complications can occur. They include infection, reactions to ink, MRI complications, dermal conditions, delayed reactions (some up to 20 years after the tattoo), and other adverse effects including hematomas, creating a burden on the lymphatic system and interference with melanoma diagnosis. These are only the medical issues.

In an article on omg.yahoo, model Niki Taylor tells about the pain of having some of her tattoos removed. Niki is quoted as saying, "The pain of the process exceeds that of childbirth,"—and she delivered twins! Because some tattoos are associated with gangs, some employers require that any tattoos be covered at all times. One of my former co-workers has to daily use sweat bands or bandages to conceal his tattoos. One of my former customers who had a large tattoo on his arm from his Navy day's decades earlier, became allergic to the tattoo and had to have multiple treatments to remove it. Our skin is actually the largest organ of our body. I think most of us have had a sunburn sometime in our lives, and we know how extremely painful that can be. We should take great consideration before we intentionally inject a foreign substance between the layers of our skin.

Possibly the most harmful thing we can do to our bodies is to smoke. Years of study have confirmed that smoking causes many forms of cancer and according to the American Cancer Society, half of all smokers who keep smoking will end up dying from a smoking-related illness. (www.cancer.org/Healthy/StayAwayfromTobacco/GuidetoQuittingSmoking). I think it would be beneficial for our older children to see the difference between the lung of a smoker and someone who doesn't smoke. Because I took anatomy, I saw those differences. God wants us to have an abundant life and to use the talents He has given us. When we have chosen to do something that reduces the life-giving oxygen to our bodies, we create poor air quality not only for ourselves, but also for those around us. I have heard that it is such a hard addiction to conquer, but those hard times are when we need to call out to God, (*I can do everything through Him who gives me strength.*" Philippians 4:13). There are many programs to help you stop smoking. Check with your local health department to see what is available to you.

I know you may be starting to feel like I'm beating you up, but all these suggestions that I'm making to you are because I care enough to talk about the hard things.

Okay, one last health subject and then I'll quit. One of the leading health problems in the U.S. is obesity. We are such a blessed nation that many of us are just carrying around too much excess calories. Our wheelbarrows are just too full and that makes it hard to haul all of it around. I have been diabetic for four years now. I have had to learn so much about calories, sugar grams and metabolism. So far I have been able to keep my sugar levels relatively stable by what I eat and do not have to do insulin injections. Because my blood sugar should not get too high or too low, I eat three small meals and three snacks per day. It takes concentrated effort, but I feel so much better and have more consistent energy levels when I eat correctly. I was only fifteen pounds overweight when I was diagnosed, but I was afraid eating six times per day would cause me to gain weight. What is so surprising to me is that in the first two years I lost the excess fifteen pounds and now have more energy and almost no problem with my one weak knee. I learned that when you skip meals, your body goes into a kind of anti-starvation mode and burns calories more slowly. Our miraculous bodies compensate for less food by slowing down the metabolism. Think about all those people in starving countries who sometimes only get one small serving of rice per day or less. We need to learn to fuel our bodies with only the calories that we will be burning. I think one of the biggest contributing factors to our obesity problem is too large portion sizes and too little movement and exercise. Think about how many of us have spent years sitting at a desk. For the first few weeks after being diagnosed, I would periodically measure what my portion size should be. It really surprised me how overly generous I was on a consistent basis guessing what my portion size should look like. I think we have lost sight of living in moderation. We have grown to believe if a little is good, a lot is even better. In Proverbs 23:20-21 it says, *"Do not join those who drink too much wine or gorge themselves on meat, for drunkards and gluttons become poor, and drowsiness clothes them in rags."* Have you ever eaten at a buffet and ate so much that all you wanted to do was go home and go to bed?

According to the dictionary, gluttony is described as, "The act or habit of eating to excess." I think we all have times of eating to excess (Thanksgiving comes to mind), but I think the key is if it is a habit. We need to not only understand how many calories we should eat and what our portion size should look like, but it does matter what we eat. Nutritious food doesn't just provide calories, but includes vitamins, minerals and fiber. We need to be aware of consuming certain things that we call empty calories. Alcohol and high sugar desserts are at the top of the list.

CHAPTER 12
CONTENTMENT & JOY

Think back to a time when you were completely content. For me, that is usually after I have accomplished something, whether it be a chore I dreaded or something I enjoyed creating. Sometimes contentment is just enjoying the beautiful mountain view from our home, or sipping a hot cup of tea while sitting by the heater and watching the snow or rain. Contentment is the feeling of quiet peace and joy that so often escapes us.

When we are content with what we have, there is an atmosphere of peace. I love what Proverbs 17:1 says, *"Better a dry crust with peace and quiet than a house full of feasting with strife."* If there isn't harmony in our home, joy has a hard time living there. So what is the opposite of harmony? It is probably contention, which is controversy, arguments, competition, rivalry, or being quarrelsome. Proverbs talks about that, too. *"Better to dwell in a corner of a housetop, than in a house shared with a contentious woman."* (Proverbs 21:9) (NKJ).

Wow, we can really make a difference in the atmosphere of our homes. Proverbs 21:19 is even more adamant, *"Better to dwell in the wilderness, than with a contentious and angry woman."*(NKJV). Does your attitude provide an oasis or a battle ground?

Now men are not excluded from this either. *"As charcoal is to burning coals, and wood to fire, so is a contentious man to kindle strife."*(Proverbs 26:21) (NKJV).

We know Jesus came to give us abundant lives, so what wisdom does the Bible give us about contentment? I think Paul makes the perfect statement regarding this. In Philippians 4:12-13 it says, *"I know what it is to be in need, and I know what it is to have plenty. I have learned the secret of being content in any and every situation, whether well fed or hungry, whether living in plenty or in want. I can do everything through Him who gives me strength."* But, Paul does add in verse 14, *"Yet it was good of you to share in my troubles."*

God will give us the strength we need to go through any circumstance, but a loving hug from a Christian sister or brother does make the load seem lighter. What joy we share when we can be the hands and feet of Jesus!

Do you seek a life that honors God? In 1Timothy 6:6-8 we are told, *"But godliness with contentment is great gain. For we brought nothing into the world, and we can take nothing out of it. But if we have food and clothing, we will be content with that."*

One of our greatest blessings is not to have war in our country. We are the land of the free because of the brave. Thank every person you meet who is serving in the military. When I went to Israel I saw first hand what life is like in a country that has never truly known peace. Because of the warring factions within the boundaries of one country, there is strife and the reality of experiencing gunfire, grenade attacks and bombs almost daily.

In addition to their inner strife, Israel is surrounded by countries that have animosity towards them and they also lack stability. Think about the neighboring countries that surround Israel. There is Lebanon, Syria, Jordan, Iraq and Egypt.

When we toured Mount Carmel, hundreds of the youth of Israel were having a field trip there. Their field trip was not going to Disneyland, the Ashland Shakespearean Festival or a ballgame. Their team competitions were to see who could carry stretchers of wounded up the mountain the fastest. For their training they used sandbags and bottles of water instead of people.

Because of their continual battle to retain their land, every Israelite has to serve in their military. The Israel Defense Forces is one of the most battle-trained armed forces in the world. Even females have to serve for two years after graduation. When we were there the pastor of the church we visited was being reactivated for a month of training activities. Men can be reactivated for at most a month every year until their mid-forties. Reservists may still volunteer after that age.

We asked our guide why all of the homes looked so similar. Their building code says that outside walls should be two feet thick and be able to withstand a grenade attack. Most of the homes are built using very similar stone. Some of the newer homes include a bomb shelter.

On September 11, 2001, when I watched the twin towers being attacked with my co-workers, I thought that life as we knew it was over. Due to the terrorist attacks, over 3,000 people died including over 400 police officers and firefighters. If not for the brave men and women who serve to protect us, our lives would be so different. The peace and safety that we enjoy is not free and should not be taken for granted. Be grateful and thank those who serve.

After spending two weeks in both Zambia and Nicaragua, there are few things I take for granted. We are so privileged just to be able to turn on a faucet for water. We don't have to haul our water like so many do daily. We even have water that is safe to drink and hot water for showers. We truly are pampered people.

Our laundry days consist of throwing our clothes into a machine. In both Zambia and Nicaragua, laundry is done daily in a tub of water, using a washboard and hung on a clothesline. In the farthest reaches from civilization, some women still go to the local streams and rivers to do their wash. A few years ago, the niece of the pastor's wife that we stayed with was killed by a crocodile when she went fishing with her father. How many things we take for granted and never appreciate! Have an attitude of gratitude.

When you go to the poor countries that have so little, you would be amazed how joyful and exuberant their church services are. They realize they have what they really need; Jesus. They do not spend hours of their day watching a television or spending time on a computer. They do their laundry together, sharing life, laughing and crying together. Their social lives are centered around their church. Their music is upbeat and joyous, though often without any instrumental accompaniment.

In Zambia, their deepest pain, just like ours, comes because of sin. In the poor compound where we visited, there are so many widows and orphans because of AIDS. When we stray from God's commandments, it is then that we harm ourselves and others.

It is when we realize how much we have that we can learn to be better stewards. By being thrifty, you will be able to have some money left over that you can use to bless others. If you only save $25 a month, that can be used to change someone's life. For just $25 a month, I now sponsor a little boy in Zambia named Teddy through Mustard Tree Ministry International that my friend Barbara and her husband established. He is such a cute, sharp little guy. He and the family he lives with can now count on monthly help to pay for his schooling and food for his family.

One of the best gifts you can give is a Bible. The word of God is love, wisdom and hope. My friend Barbara is working with the Gideons International organization to provide more Bibles for the children and families in Zambia written in their own language.

Other worthy organizations are those that provide clean drinking water to people who need it around the world. When you give the gift of water, people are also open to receive the Living Water in the Bible.

We are not just floating through time and chaos with no end in sight. We know there is a God who loves us dearly. The Creator of the universe loves you and me, and has plans for us. We have the ultimate hero who tells us, *"Keep your lives free from the love of money and be content with what you have, because God has said, "Never will I leave you; never will I forsake you."* (Hebrews 13:5).

When we have grown to love and trust our God and Savior Jesus, and realize that the Holy Spirit lives within us; we are safe in the cleft of the Rock and our foundation is firm in all storms. In Proverbs 19:23 we read, *"The fear of the LORD leads to life: Then one rests content, untouched by trouble."*

What brings joy to your heart? I know that a beautiful song with just the right lyrics can change my attitude and my day. Music is a soothing balm to my soul. I so look forward to the worship team in our church leading us in songs of love to God. In Chronicles when it was describing the Ark of the Covenant being brought to Jerusalem we read, *"Then David spoke to the leaders of the Levites to appoint their brethren to be the singers accompanied by instruments of music, stringed instruments, harps, and cymbals, by raising the voice with resounding joy."* (1 Chronicles 15:16) (NKJV). They were celebrating the presence of God being with them.

We have the possibility of joy every day of our lives. Did you notice that singing and music was not dull and sedate? It had harps and cymbals and there was resounding joy. I have the joy of joining in that celebration with the saints every Sunday. I cannot imagine missing that boost of weekly joy. Sometimes when we are down or sad, we may not feel like going to church or being around other people. Uplifting music in the praise of our God can clear many a dark cloud away. The Bible tells us, *"The LORD is my strength and my shield; my heart trusts in him, and I am helped. My heart leaps for joy and I will give thanks to him in song."* (Psalm 28:7).

Do you ever feel overwhelmed by people in your life who seem to continually bring you down? Have you tried everything, and think nothing changes? We serve a God who is in control. In Ezra 6:22 we read how God changed the attitude of the king of Assyria. *"For seven days they celebrated with joy the Feast of Unleavened Bread, because the LORD had filled them with joy by changing the attitude of the king of Assyria, so that he assisted them in the work on the house of God, the God of Israel."*

God can and does use people who are not His followers. The Bible even tells us how one time God used a donkey to speak to Balaam (a pagan prophet) who was trying to resist God. Numbers 22:28 reads, *"Then the Lord opened the donkey's mouth, and she said to Balaam, "What have I done to you to make you beat me these three times?"* The donkey had seen the angel of the Lord blocking the narrow path and had laid down refusing to go forward. It wasn't until the donkey reasoned with Balaam that Balaam saw the angel of the Lord standing in the road with his sword drawn.

God can use anyone or anything to accomplish His good will. God is so faithful and loving that He does not want anyone to perish.

If you have not discovered this already, there are people that refuse to be "fixed or changed". A change of heart can only come from God. However, the Bible gives us guidance in all circumstances. In 1 Peter 3:1-2 we learn, *"Wives, in the same way be submissive to your husbands so that, if any of them do not believe the word, they may be won over without words by the behavior of their wives, when they see the purity and reverence of your lives."* I love the song lyrics that say, "I'd rather see a sermon than to hear one any day." Amen. Lord, help us to do this daily.

Do you sometimes feel that those not following God seem to be doing fine? Job 20:4-5 tells us, *"Surely you know how it has been from of old, ever since man was placed on the earth, that the mirth of the wicked is brief, the joy of the godless lasts but a moment."* We serve a just God who will see to it that the wicked are punished and the righteous are rewarded.

How do we have joy when daily we see Satan seeming to triumph over the saints? We can choose how we will live our lives. We either accept God's laws or we reject them. When you keep God's laws, you can sleep with a clear conscience knowing you have done your best to do the right thing. *"The precepts* [standards or guide to morals] *of the LORD are right, giving joy to the heart. The commands of the LORD are radiant, giving light to the eyes."* (Psalm 19:8).

Being light in a dark world is what should set us apart. There is a reward waiting for us. *"Surely you have granted him eternal blessings and made him glad with the joy of your presence."* (Psalm 21:6). If you want to have no regrets and be able to see your reflection with no shame, do what is right. *"There is deceit in the hearts of those who plot evil, but joy for those who promote peace."* (Proverbs 12:20).

There are times when those we love are not aware of the trials we are suffering or are not able to be with us. The awesome part of being a child of God is knowing that He is always with us. He is with us anytime and anywhere, *"When anxiety was great within me, your consolation brought joy to my soul."* (Psalm 94:19).

Do you ever feel like a small, weak, insignificant person who probably will not accomplish much in your life? Our true strength comes not from us, but from God. There are many stories in the Bible about God's small army conquering much larger ones. In Luke chapter 10, we read about Jesus sending out seventy-two other disciples two by two ahead of him to every place where he was about to go. In verse 17 we read, *"The seventy-two returned with joy and said, "Lord, even the demons submit to us in your name."*

There is no power greater than God, and if you have accepted Jesus as your Savior, His power is with you and within you.

Sometimes in life you may feel alone. We moved often due to my step-dad being a heavy equipment operator. We moved from job to job, sometimes two or three times a year. It seemed like we would just settle in and make new friends, and then it was time to move again.

When we left Brazil, Indiana, I made a decision that I would like wherever we lived and find something beautiful about the area. I have lived in over 20 different places, and God is truly everywhere you go and there are kind people in every location. Whether we were in Nenana, Alaska or Brownsville, Texas; there was beauty and an amazing variety of people, plants and scenery.

To have friends, you must be a friend. Whether it was a neighbor, fellow student or Christian from church; God placed wonderful people in my life. I learned to love unconditionally and immediately and then like freeing a beautiful bird, remembered them fondly when we left. It was hard, but it was better than not taking the chance to be friendly and possibly missing out on making another friend.

I have been blessed with a few friendships that have lasted my lifetime. We all seem to instinctively know that when we can be together, we love it; but when we can't, we accept it. I have learned to bloom wherever God plants me. Sometimes I wished we could have had a life with less moving, but now that I am older I realize the many blessings I gained. I know a man that never went outside the county that he was born in. When I think of all the different scenery, climates and cultures I've experienced, I know God exposed me to many adventures that have given me such a rich variety in my life.

The one constant that has always been with me is Jesus. In John 15:14-17, Jesus calls us His friends. Wow, what better friend could you have? *"You are my friends if you do what I command. I no longer call you servants, because a servant does not know his master's business. Instead, I have called you friends, for everything that I learned from my Father I have made known to you. You did not choose me, but I chose you and appointed you to go and bear fruit—fruit that will last. Then the Father will give you whatever you ask in my name. This is my command: Love each other."* The Son of God is my friend. I am blessed wherever I am. Thank you, Jesus.

If I didn't walk with Jesus, I would probably be very sad at times. As we age, sometimes those things we enjoyed doing most, can no longer be done. There is daily pain and people are so busy that there's not always time to stay in touch. But, that's okay. As each day passes, we are that much closer to an eternity in heaven with no more sickness, no more tears, and no more death.

I can tell you that fifty plus years have gone by in a flash. However many years I have left and whatever illness or pain may follow, I still have a bright future to which I can look forward. It is better than a pot of gold at the end of a rainbow. John 16:22 tells us, *"So with you: Now is your time of grief, but I will see you again and you will rejoice, and no one will take away your joy."*

As Christians, our future is guaranteed and our mansion is waiting in heaven. In our final days on earth, how should we live? *"Be joyful in hope, patient in affliction, faithful in prayer."* (Romans 12:12). Wow, that's a tall order. How do we do that? *"May the God of hope fill you with all joy and peace as you trust in him, so that you may overflow with hope by the power of the Holy Spirit."* (Romans 15:13). We don't even have to call for Him to help us, He is always with us.

There is a song called, "They'll Know We are Christians by Our Love." We are supposed to be different, set apart for God. Paul gives us a great set of marching orders. *"Be joyful always; pray continually; give thanks in all circumstances, for this is God's will for you in Christ Jesus."* (1 Thessalonians 5:16-18).

May you be content and joyful knowing you are a child of God, dearly loved. Count your blessings and have an attitude of gratitude. Your Father has great plans for you now and for eternity.

CHAPTER 13
DARE TO CARE

Because the greatest commandments are to love God and to love others, we should consider how we can best love God and others. The fruit of the Spirit should be evident in our lives (love, joy, peace, patience, kindness, goodness, faithfulness, gentleness, and self-control). If we can consciously include those things in our character, then our field of service will contain an infinite amount of possibilities to love and serve others.

When a family member or friend is in crisis, it may feel awkward to step in to try to love and console them. A true friend is one who rushes in when others are rushing out. You may have been told to stay out of other people's business, and that is true if you are only curious and not concerned. In Philippians 2:4 it says, *"Each of you should look not only to your own interests, but also to the interests of others."*

Each decision you make should also take into consideration how it will affect those around you. We are not supposed to live in a bubble or be a lone-ranger Christian.

I have known three young ladies in my life who have committed suicide. Stepping into someone else's pain may seem too bold or like you are invading their privacy. If you gently let them know that you are available to talk with them, if and whenever they might feel like it, you have given them the control of letting you in or having you wait until they are ready; or they can let you know they are not open to that. You have at least let them know that you care and if they need a listening ear, you are available.

The Bible tells us in Romans 12:15, *"Rejoice with those who rejoice; mourn with those who mourn."* Some major crisis may require a trained professional. However, it helps to know someone cares about you and what you are going through. Whenever someone confides in you, it should always remain confidential. Loose lips sink ships and others' confidence in you. There is a big difference between being a good friend and a busybody. 1 Timothy 5:13 tells us, *". . . They get into the habit of being idle and going about from house to house. And not only do they become idlers, but also gossips and busybodies, saying things they ought not to."*

I let something said in confidence slip out once, and I know it caused a lack of trust. I have never forgotten how badly I felt when I was confronted with what I had done. There are so many positive things about God to talk about without ever conversing about anyone else.

Besides asking someone what you could do for them, you can suggest ways you would like to help them. You can say, "I could bring you a meal on Friday or I could come over and vacuum this weekend." It is hard for most people to accept help, because we realize that everyone is busy and have plenty to do themselves.

When we suggest specific ways we would like to help them, it gives them options that they know we feel comfortable doing.

Some people love to cook and some people hate to cook. When you state what you can do, they know you are open to that need. Service really means to see a need and fill it. When you do for others, you will receive the best blessing when you do it without any recognition. In Matthew 6:1 Jesus said, *"Be careful not to do your' acts of righteousness' before men, to be seen by them. If you do, you will have no reward from your Father in heaven."*

God has given lavishly to us. He is proud of us when we do that for others. Jesus tells us in Matthew 5:41, *"If someone forces you to go one mile, go with him two miles."* In 2 Corinthian 9:7 Paul said, *"Each man should give what he has decided in his heart to give, not reluctantly or under compulsion, for God loves a cheerful giver."*

When we do something begrudgingly, it is apparent that our heart is not in the act. When our hearts are softened, we begin to yearn to serve. God does not ask us to give what we do not have. When your children are small or you are a caregiver, there may be times you do not have the time or the energy to do for others beyond your own family. God sees that and understands.

We have to have balance and boundaries in our lives. 1 Corinthians 14:33 says, *"For God is not a God of disorder but of peace . . ."* This verse is referring to the church, but I believe this should also be true of our homes. There is a hierarchy of responsibility. God should come first, then your family and then your community. In 1 Timothy 5:8 it says, *"If anyone does not provide for his relatives, and especially for his immediate family, he has denied the faith and is worse than an unbeliever."*

There are times when we should say no. In 2 Thessalonians 3:10 it says, *"For even when we were with you, we gave you this rule: "If a man will not work, he shall not eat."* You may have heard the term, "tough love". This is what we sometimes must do to make an irresponsible person stand on their own two feet and pull their own weight. It is not good to allow someone to always depend on you to bail them out. It is not beneficial to them to repeatedly let them be careless with their finances.

As children we relied on our parents to support us. As we become adults, we should be independent and self-sufficient. There comes a time when parents are no longer able to help or they die. It is better sooner than later to learn to save for unexpected emergencies and spend less than you earn. Proverbs 22:6 says, *"Train a child in the way he should go, and when he is old he will not turn from it."*

In talking about being a good steward, Jesus said, *"Whoever can be trusted with very little can also be trusted with much, and whoever is dishonest with very little will also be dishonest with much. So if you have not been trustworthy in handling worldly wealth, who will trust you with true riches? And if you have not been trustworthy with someone else's property, who will give you property of your own?"* (Luke 16:10-12). People usually will not change bad habits if they do not suffer the consequences of their poor choices.

CHAPTER 14
WHAT WAS I THINKING?

Many years ago during Bible study at a church campout, we read one of the verses that referred to the saints. I wasn't exactly sure who "the saints" were, so I asked our pastor. He asked me if I had accepted Jesus as my savior and if I was trying to live my life as God directed. I answered yes to both questions. Then the pastor said, "That makes you one of the saints, saint Michele." I had never thought of myself as a saint, and I was both elated and humbled by the thought. It made me look at myself and the way I lived life differently. In life, we can accept a label we have received or reject it. I sincerely want to live life guided by God's love and wisdom; but that requires learning exactly what God requires.

The hardest part for me in following God's commands is controlling my thoughts. Saying kind words or performing acts of service seem to come easier with years of practice; but, what is still a struggle for me is my thought life. In 2 Corinthians 10:5 we read, "*We demolish arguments and every pretension that sets itself up against the knowledge of God, and we take captive every thought to make it obedient to Christ.*" When I see that phrase "take captive", I think about something entering my mind that shouldn't be there, grabbing it and yelling, "Gotcha!". I find that just throwing it out is not enough. I need to replace that errant thought with something positive. There is an old saying that, "Idle hands are the devil's tools." I think an idle mind that does not have boundaries can go where we should not be. In 1 Timothy 5:13 we read, *"Besides, they get into the habit of being idle and going about from house to house. And not only do they become idlers, but also gossips and busybodies, saying things they ought not to."* What we are thinking often determines our actions. If we don't stop thoughts that are going in the wrong direction, it is possible we will act on them. As the old saying goes, "One bad apple spoils the whole barrel." Psalm 10:4 says, *"In his pride the wicked does not seek him; in all his thoughts there is no room for God."* We need to push out what should not have come in and replace it with godly thoughts.

God gives us great guidelines to tell us what we should be thinking about. In Philippians 4:8 we are told, *"Finally, brothers, whatever is true, whatever is noble, whatever is right, whatever is pure, whatever is lovely, whatever is admirable—if anything is excellent or praiseworthy—think about such things."*

My mom used to tell us, "If you can't say something nice, don't say anything at all." That is good advice; however, even thinking about or dwelling on things that are not right is a sin. In Hebrews 4:12-13 we read, *"For the word of God is living and active. Sharper than any double-edged sword, it penetrates even to dividing soul and* *spirit, joints and marrow; it judges the **thoughts** and **attitudes** of the heart. Nothing in all creation is hidden from God's sight. Everything is uncovered and laid bare before the eyes of him to who we must give account."*

If you think it doesn't matter what you think as long as you don't say it or act on that thought, read what Jesus said. Jesus tells us in Matthew 5:27-28, *"You have heard that it was said, "Do not commit adultery. But I tell you that anyone who looks at a woman lustfully has already committed adultery with her in his heart."* How can we live godly lives in an ungodly world? We are not responsible for the world, but we are responsible for how we live our lives and how we train our children. We should make a conscious effort not to be a stumbling block to others. We should dress modestly and keep our "private parts" private. When I was working, it was one of my duties to discuss job guidelines with new employees. It surprised me that I had to counsel new employees that cleavage and posterior cracks were to be covered in the work environment.

There are times when I struggle to stop thinking about words people have spoken that hurt me so I could forgive them and let go of the pain and anger. I know not dwelling on them would help, but my mind just keeps unburying those thoughts that I want to blot out.

In Chapter 3, I told the story about David and the forgiveness that he earnestly desired. In Psalm 51 David pours out his heart to God. David was tortured by his sins and cried out to God. A telling statement that showed his torment was in verse 3 when he wrote, *"For I know my transgressions, and my sin is always before me."*

David had tried to escape his guilt and shame, but was haunted by it. David needed God to accomplish what David could not do for himself. You will be blessed by reading the story in chapters 11 and 12 of 2 Samuel and learning how David received the forgiveness and cleansing that he desired. In Psalm 51:10, we read, *"Create in me a pure heart, O god, and renew a steadfast spirit within me."* David also asks for help and guidance in Psalm 19:14 when he writes, *"May the words of my mouth and the meditation of my heart be pleasing in your sight, O Lord, my Rock and my Redeemer."* David asked to be held accountable by God. Our close friends can also help us with accountability to do and think about what is right.

When we become fixated on something we shouldn't think about, we need to choose to think about something that is beneficial. In 2 Peter 3:1 it says, *"Dear friends, this is now my second letter to you. I have written both of them as reminders to stimulate you to wholesome thinking."* Peter continues in verse 2 to tell us what we should be thinking about. *"I want you to recall the words spoken in the past by the holy prophets and the command given by our Lord and Savior through your apostles."* I always try to have a stack of books waiting to be read that are by Christian authors or have been highly recommended. Many of the books I purchase come from our library when they have their fundraisers. All of them are a dollar or less. Some books I return to our used bookstore and receive a credit to buy more books. The books I think are especially helpful are kept. I now have two bookcases that are full.

Trade books with friends and then you can have great discussions about what each of you learned.

Another great way to stop your gnawing thoughts is to listen to inspirational music. Remember how David soothed King Saul? *"And so it was, whenever the spirit from God was upon Saul, that David would take a harp and play it with his hand. Then Saul would become refreshed and well, and the distressing spirit would depart from him."* (1 Samuel 16:23) (NKJV).

We have a wonderful Christian radio station that carries not just uplifting music, but also outstanding Christian speakers. It's definitely my station of choice. When I walk, I usually listen to my ipod that is almost entirely Christian music. One of the benefits of finding songs to sing at the mission is that I have a great collection of music.

An idle mind or one without boundaries and direction can be the weak link where wrong thoughts and attitudes can enter our lives. If our relationship with the person we are having a problem with is positive enough, it is good to talk to that person. If a conversation can't happen in a positive way, a letter to them could be a better way to handle the problem. If someone who you have struggled with enters your mind, that is the time to pray for them and their family. When we pray to God for someone, it causes us to seek God's love and wisdom for them. By praying for positive results in someone's life, it causes us to create positive thoughts about them. In the book, The Hiding Place, as Betsy's health steadily declines from life in the concentration camp; Betsy describes to Corrie how she wants to create a home for their persecutors to show and teach them the love of God. Most of us do not see people who hurt us or persecute us with such grace and mercy. Only God's love and wisdom can produce an attitude and life that has that much grace and mercy. Thank you, God, for giving us your strength and love for others beyond what we can do on our own.

CHAPTER 15
YOUR SAVIOR, MENTOR & FRIEND

It is wonderful to have a good friend and mentor, but people cannot always be there when you need them; Jesus can. The Bible tells us that we should grow up and mature as Christians. The only way to learn to keep God's commandments and live as Jesus modeled for us, is to study the Bible and take those words to heart. I love being a mother, friend and mentor; but the best advice I can give to you is to study the Bible. There is no person as wise and loving as God. There is not one person who has lived a perfect life on earth except Jesus.

I love Sunday mornings and being able to gather with my Christian sisters and brothers. I love that so many of the songs we sing are worded so we are singing directly to God, Jesus and the Holy Spirit. It is so meaningful if you can close your eyes and sing directly to the holy Trinity. I know I like to hear "Thank you." and "I love you." I'm sure God does, too.

The times I have felt closest to God were when I was alone with no television or radio to distract my thoughts. I usually start by thanking God for the many blessings I have in my life. When we consider all that God, Jesus and the Holy Spirit do for us moment by moment, then we can't help but feel a love and gratitude for the wonders that God provides.

Next I pour out my heart to God about anyone or anything that is on my heart. I know I lack insight about the big picture of life, so I always ask for His love and wisdom in my life. When I pray for others, I always ask that God would open their hearts and minds to His guidance, that God would put good role models and mentors in their lives, that they would be led to a good Bible teaching church family, and that they would be open to follow God's path for their lives.

It is so amazing to me that God wants a relationship with us. When Jesus taught us how we should pray, this is what He said: *"Our Father in heaven, hallowed be your name, your kingdom come, your will be done on earth as it is in heaven. Give us today our daily bread. Forgive us our debts, as we also have forgiven our debtors. And lead us not into temptation, but deliver us from the evil one."* (Matthew 6:9-13).

God is the ultimate Father that we all wished we had on earth. He let His only Son come to earth, show us how to live, and die to pay for our sins. There is no love greater than the love that God has for each one of us.

The final words I leave with you are the words Paul left with the Thessalonians. *"Now we ask you, brothers, to respect those who work hard among you, who are over you in the Lord and who admonish you. Hold them in the highest regard in love because of their work. Live in peace with each other. And we urge you, brothers, warn those who are idle, encourage the timid, help the weak, be patient with everyone. Make sure that nobody pays back wrong for wrong, but always try to be kind to each other and to everyone else."*

"Be joyful always; pray continually; give thanks in all circumstances, for this is God's will for you in Christ Jesus."

Amen [so be it].

NOTES

Chapter 1

1. *NIV Study Bible,* (Grand Rapids, Michigan: Zondervan, 1984), p. 1470. All verses used are from the NIV Study Bible, 1984 unless otherwise noted.

Chapter 10

1. Dr. Emerson & Sarah Eggerichs, *Love & Respect Marriage Conference,* (Grand Rapids: Thomas Nelson, 2004)

2. Funk & Wagnalls Standard Encyclopedic Dictionary (Chicago: J.G. Ferguson Publishing Company, 1972)

Chapter 11

1. Joni Eareckson Tada, *Joni: An Unforgettable Story,* (Grand Rapids: Zondervan, 2001)

2. *Taber's Cyclopedic Medical Dictionary,* (Philadelphia: F.A. Davis Company, 1986) p. 943.

3. Corrie Ten Boom and John and Elizabeth Sherrill, *The Hiding Place*, (Old Tappan: A Bantam Book/arrangement with Fleming H. Revell Company, 1974)

4. Pastor Richard Wurmbrand, *Tortured for Christ*, (Bartlesville: Living Sacrifice Book Company, 1998)

5. Brother Yun, *The Heavenly Man*, (Grand Rapids: Monarch Books, 2002)

6. Barbara Johnson, *Stick a Geranium in Your Hat and Be Happy!* (Nashville: Thomas Nelson, 2004), p.3.

7. Dr. Emerson & Sarah Eggerichs, *Love & Respect*, (Grand Rapids: Love & Respect Ministries Studio, 2006) www.loveandrespect.com.

8. *Standard Encyclopedic Dictionary*, (Chicago: J.G. Ferguson Publishing Company, 1972) p. 203.

ABBREVIATIONS

NKJ   New King James

NKJV New King James Version

NLT   New Living Translation

RESOURCES

Books

Eugene H. Peterson, *The Message, The Bible in Contemporary Language*, (Colorado Springs: Navpress, 2002)

Leslie Vernick, *How to Act Right When Your Spouse Acts Wrong*, (Colorado Springs: Waterbrook Press, 2009)

Dr. Henry Cloud and Dr. John Townsend, *Boundaries, When to Say Yes, When to Say No, To Take Control of Your Life*, (Grand Rapids: Zondervan, 1992)

Johann Christoph Arnold, *Why Forgive?*, (Rifton: The Plough Publishing House of Church Communities International, 2010)

Websites

themustardtreeministry.org—Mustard Tree Ministry International (help for orphans and widows)

mintools.com—Ministry Tools (Spiritual Gifts)

loveandrespect.com—Marriage

kvip.org—Christian music and programing

waterandstone.org—Clean water

BibleGateway.com—Bible/Search, lookup, index

blueletterbible.org—Bible/Dictionary Search

JoniandFriends.org—International Disability Center

FocusontheFamily.com—Helping Families Thrive

Helpguide.org—Help for Health challenges (Cutting & Self-harm), Addictions, Mental Health, Healthy Lifestyles, Children & Family, Aging Well

Gideons.org—Distributing Bibles and New Testaments around the World

Cancer.org—Guide to Quitting Smoking

Songs

All Across the Sky—The Faith Crew

Count Your Blessings—Don Marsh

Creation Calls—Brian Doerksen

Do Not Be Afraid—Acappella

Follow You—Leeland

Friends—Michael W. Smith

Garbage In, Garbage Out—Tal & Acacia

He Will Love You—Cheri Keaggy

His Eye Is on the Sparrow—Sandi Patty

His Mercies Are New Every Morning—Taranda Greene

I'll Fly Away—Larry Gatlin

I Lift Up My Eyes—Scripture Memory Songs

I Love You All the Time—Daniel Markoya

It Doesn't Matter—New Desire

Jesus Loves Me—The Wonder Kids

Jesus Loves the Little Children—The Christian Children's Choir

Oh, How He Loves You and Me—Don Marsh Singers

One Day at a Time—Cristy Lane

Thank You for Giving to the Lord—African Gospel Rhythms

They'll Know We Are Christians By Our Love—Jars of Clay

Through It All—Carroll Roberson

Whatever Is True—Rescue